W9-BNH-172

Asheville

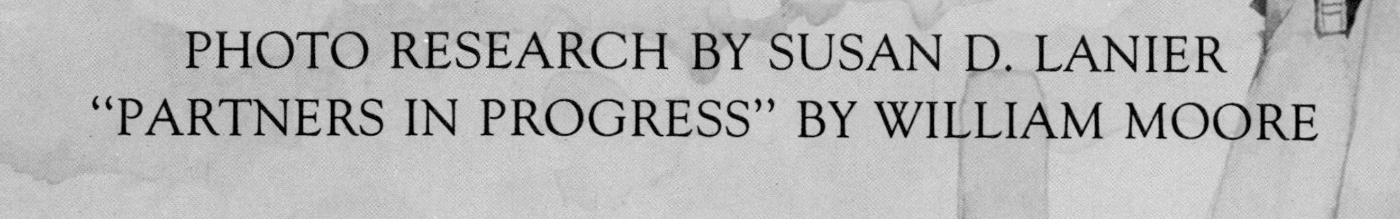

PHOTO RESEARCH BY SUSAN D. LANIER
"PARTNERS IN PROGRESS" BY WILLIAM MOORE

PRODUCED IN COOPERATION WITH
THE WESTERN NORTH CAROLINA
HISTORICAL ASSOCIATION
WINDSOR PUBLICATIONS, INC.
NORTHRIDGE, CALIFORNIA

Asheville
LAND OF THE SKY

An Illustrated History By Milton Ready

For my parents, Bud and Ella Ready

Endsheets: *A meteorological signal station was built on Mitchell's Peak, and food and supplies for the men who lived and worked there were packed in from ten miles away. This 1870s photo is titled "Breakfast Time on Mitchell." Courtesy, North Carolina Department of Archives and History (NCDAH)*

Previous pages: *Located in the heart of Asheville, the old Battery Park Hotel stood on an oak-covered hill extending twenty-five acres. Erected in 1886 by Colonel Frank Coxe, the hotel accommodated wealthy guests from all over the world. Margaret Y. Locke captured the beauty of the hotel in a watercolor in 1985. Courtesy, Margaret Y. Locke*

Facing page: *Known as Asheville's playground, Recreation Park was created during the boom period, circa 1927. Located along the Swannanoa River, the park offered Asheville's residents a swimming pool, golf course, zoo, bowling alley, Ferris wheel, rides, dances several nights a week, and a lake for boat rides. Lake Craig was drained in the 1950s due to the accumulation of silt. Courtesy, Ewart Ball Collection, Southern Highlands, UNC-Asheville*

Windsor Publications—History Books Division
Publisher: John M. Phillips
Editorial Director: Teri Davis Greenberg
Design Director: Alexander D'Anca

Staff for *Asheville: Land of the Sky*
Senior Editor: Julie Jaskol
Editor: Marilyn Horn
Director, Corporate Biographies: Karen Story
Assistant Director, Corporate Biographies: Phyllis Gray
Editor, Corporate Biographies: Judy Hunter
Production Editor, Corporate Biographies: Una FitzSimmons
Layout Artist, Corporate Biographies: Mari Catherine Preimesberger
Sales Representative, Corporate Biographies: William Harrison
Editorial Assistants: Kathy M. Brown, Laura Cordova, Marcie Goldstein, Pam Juneman, Pat Pittman
Proofreader: Susan Muhler
Design and Layout: Ellen Ifrah

Library of Congress Cataloging-in-Publication Data

Ready, Milton, 1938-
Asheville: land of the sky.

Bibliography: p. 134
Includes index.
1. Asheville (N.C.)—History. 2. Asheville (N.C.)—Description. 3. Asheville (N.C.)—Industries. I. Title
F264.A8R43 1986 975.6'88 86-23368
ISBN 0-89781-168-2

Honorary Advisors

Dr. William Highsmith
Jerry Birdwell
F. Ed Broadwell, Jr.
Dr. David Brown
Robert F. Burgin
Jerry L. Cole
Frank Coxe
John N. Daniel
Claude M. Drake
E. Charles Dyson
Durward R. Everett, Jr.
Robert W. Helms
Dr. Reuben A. Holden
Sidney A. Hughes
Dr. Donald D. Jones
Gerry Kitch
The Honorable Larry McDevitt
Dr. N.A. Miller
Ralph D. Morris, Jr.
Tom Morrisey
William O. Prescott
Charles Price
R. Curtis Ratcliff
Sister Mary Veronica Schumacher
Sheldon A. Summerlin
L.T. Ward
Maurice H. Winger, Jr.
Richard A. Wood, Jr.

Windsor Publications and the Western North Carolina Historical Association wish to thank these individuals for their valuable assistance in the preparation of this book.

CONTENTS

Facing page: *"Mountain Memories" is the title of a series of oil paintings by Cleo Williams of Marble, North Carolina.* "Doing the Wash *is a composition from my own imagination. . . . The lady doing the wash makes one remember other things—the rub board and the strong brown soap, the old bench where the tubs sat, the smell of wood smoke and the fresh scent of the clothes while taking them from the line after hanging in the sun all day. Then came the ironing with the black irons heated on the wood stove."* Courtesy, Cleo Williams

ACKNOWLEDGMENTS

I first want to thank three people whose efforts helped make this book possible. William Highsmith, chancellor emeritus of the University of North Carolina at Asheville and past president of the Western North Carolina Historical Society, recommended me as the author. I know of no one whose life has been more dedicated to the community he has served so well and loved so much for more than two decades. Susan Lanier, photographer and artist, gave me a greater visual appreciation of Asheville and its architectural past and present. Barbara Harlow did a great deal to shape the book through her research and literary interests. She also edited and word-processed the entire manuscript.

Pack Memorial Library and its staff, especially Ed Epstein, deserve special mention for their helpfulness and cooperation. Along with the Southern Highlands Research Center of the University of North Carolina at Asheville, Pack's special collections furnished much of the research material for my writing.

Two very special ladies, Frances McDowell and Rudy Camblos, kindled my interest in Asheville's history through their work with the Smith-McDowell Museum and the Western North Carolina Historical Association. To a great degree, both have kept history alive and well in Western North Carolina through their largely overlooked work. My wife, Sylvia, patiently read all my jumbled notes and, with an unfailing reader's eye, brought order and arrangement to them. Lastly, I would like to acknowledge my debt to Dr. Francis Hulme, poet, gentleman, scholar, and historian. His life was a model for us all.

Milton Ready

I must thank Dr. Milton Ready for recommending me as photo researcher. His historical expertise was invaluable in my search for information and photographs. His assistants at the Southern Highlands Research Center, Barbara Harlow and Keith Jarrett, were constantly there, supplying negatives, prints, and help with research.

Tim Barnwell, Steve Mann, and Joe Rathburn of the Appalachian Photographic Workshop spent endless hours copying and printing all the photographs for the book.

The North Carolina Collection of Pack Memorial Library offered an extensive selection of photographs. With the help of Ed Epstein, Lewis Buck, and Philip Banks I found many unique old prints.

My parents, Hollis and Nancy Craven, and my sisters Jeanne and Rhonda were constant support and encouragement. A special thanks to Lhea.

Susan D. Lanier

CHAPTER I

Garden of Eden

Facing page: *As an undiscovered Garden of Eden, Western North Carolina's natural beauty has attracted botanists, tourists, and outsiders for more than 200 years. Courtesy, Ewart Ball Collection, Southern Highlands, UNC-Asheville*

The mountains surrounding the long wide valley of the French Broad River in Western North Carolina are as old as time itself. Long before there was a place called Asheville, antedating by millions of years man's first appearance in Western North Carolina, a vast, shallow, warm sea washed over the area. There were no mountains. There was only a plateau surrounding an enormous ditch, an Appalachian trough stretching from western New York to southern Alabama. To the east and west the land rose gently to form enormous ridges bordering the inland sea.

From the almost continuous soft rain that fell 300 million years ago, huge, sluggish rivers formed to carry sediment into the great Appalachian canal. Three vast, 100-mile wide deltas were created, of which the French Broad and Tennessee rivers are remnants. For millions of years more than 25,000 feet of limestone, sandstone, shale, and other residue accumulated in the Appalachian depression, and its enormous weight frequently caused the great trough to sink. Gradually it collapsed an incredible six to eight miles into the earth's soft crust. There the original hard rock came into contact with temperatures high enough to melt and change the rock.

The resultant melting of many of the lower rock formations caused the earth above to shift and fold, creating majestic mountains. They would probably tower five miles or more above the present French Broad plain, not unlike the rugged Himalayas.

Eastern North America then passed through a slow and steady ice age. Animals did not flee before the advancing ice and snow; instead they moved with the warmth as the colder climate shifted slowly southward. To the mountains of Western North Carolina and Virginia there came giant mammoths and mastodons, various kinds of early buffalo, horses, huge pig-like animals with short tusks called peccaries, panthers, and sabre-toothed tigers. Along with them came many animals similar to those living in the area today, such as black bear and deer. In addition, arctic animals akin to the musk ox, mammoth, and walrus migrated as far south as the Carolinas and Florida.

In about 11,000 B.C., the ice and snow began to retreat for the last time. Vegetational patterns altered once again. Animals such as the musk ox and the mastodon followed the ice floes northward. Others like the bear, buffalo, and panther remained behind, the smaller varieties flourishing on the margins of the forests near the cane brakes of the Tennessee and French Broad rivers.

Facing page: *Asheville's many spring-fed streams lured tourists to relax in the area's health resorts. Photograph by Susan Lanier*

Above: *Winter brings a hushed and tranquil beauty to the area's mountains. Photograph by Susan Lanier*

Reborn after the last ice age, the forests of Western North Carolina waited several millennia for man to live in them. With over fifty species, pines flourished everywhere. From the piedmont inland, a vast, seemingly unbroken forest of pine and summer-green trees stretched to the horizon. Willow, poplar, birch, elm, mulberry, and sassafras could be found, sometimes with climbing bittersweet, grape, and creeper vines entwined around their trunks. Even the ancestor of the mighty oak, the king of North Carolina's forest today, grew in that phantom forest of long ago.

Nestled in the heart of the mountains was an undulating plateau watered by a river of placid beauty. To the first explorers, it was the Garden of Eden. The Cherokees called the river "Tah-kee-os-tee," Racing Waters, and located villages and burial grounds among the hills along the stream after it came down from "Nah-tah-ne-oh," The Place Where it Became Warm. Today, the river is called the French Broad; the town, Hot Springs.

When the first Indians and Europeans came to Western North Carolina, they encountered animal and bird life rich beyond imagination in both numbers and varieties. Including the golden eagle, well over 200 bird species were native to the region. Tanagers and swifts, owls and swallows, eagles and hawks, vultures and turkeys, parakeets and songbirds—all flourished on the land and in the air above the French Broad valley.

Facing page, far left: *According to Indian legend, Paint Rock received its name from the tint of the rock, believed at one time to be Indian symbols. (NCDAH)*

Facing page, left: *Attracted to the Asheville area by the surrounding mountains, waterfalls, and cool summertime climate, tourists made daily excursions to Craggy Gardens and Mt. Mitchell. The local hotels and inns used the beautiful mountain scenes as advertisements for their organized day trips. (NCDAH)*

Perhaps the greatest bird population of all was the now extinct passenger pigeon. Early settlers in the valleys of the French Broad, Tennessee, and Swannanoa rivers would pause in amazement at the sheer number of pigeons that flew over. Hordes of them sometimes took twelve or fourteen hours to pass down the river valleys. Each flock was at least a mile wide and one flock flew after another, several layers deep. A single flyover of one day's duration involved scores of millions of pigeons.

Settlers in Western North Carolina killed pigeons indiscriminately. Birds were roasted and packed in barrels and pickled. Breast of pigeon pickled in apple cider was a delicacy to early mountaineers. Along the French Broad and Tennessee farmers put up the fat of pigeons in tubs. It lasted for months and was described as being sweeter than butter. Invaluable to the end, the carcasses were fed to a growing hog population in the 1820s.

The passenger pigeon disappeared from Western North Carolina before 1900. When the railroad came in the 1880s, sportsmen from the piedmont and the northeast would pick up their shotguns and head for the nearest roosting. Guns, nets, cork soaked in alcohol, fire, and stool pigeons—all were used to kill every squab and adult in the French Broad River valley. The pigeon was no more, but beaver and elk persisted throughout the French Broad valley into historic times. The beaver held his own until the white man came. The sparse Indian population trapped or otherwise killed him, using him for medicine, keeping warm with peltry, and eating the tender and succulent flesh, roasted over a fire while still in the skin. Coming in large numbers in the 1760s, whites settled in the valleys and along the streams where the beaver lived. Gone from along the Swannanoa, French Broad, and the smaller streams by 1790, the beaver ceased to exist in Western North Carolina by 1803.

Driven higher up into the mountains by trappers and settlers, elk continued to roam the Blue Ridge until the early decades of the nineteenth century. John Ledere, a German physician from Virginia who traveled and trapped the area in 1670, told fantastic stories of beaver, elk, lions, and tigers in the Western Carolinas.

The romance of Western North Carolina as the Garden of Eden was perpetuated in the stories of early travelers. Virginian George Chicken wandered throughout the region in 1690. He excitedly noted finding "seven sorts of ore or mineral stones," including gold, in the mountains of the Carolinas. John Brickell, another Virginian, took a trip to the "Cherokee Mountains" in February 1730, describing an almost impossible journey across the ridges into a "Broad River valley between the mountains."

Intrigued by descriptions of William Bartram's travels through the Carolinas in 1776, Andre Michaux, a French botanist, was convinced that the New World's Garden of Eden lay in the intermontane valleys of

Above: *The view from Mt. Mitchell overlooks the North Fork Reservoir. Photo by Cotter/Carol & Adrian Cotter*

Facing page, right: *Dawn breaks in Asheville, as seen from the Mills Valley Overlook on the Blue Ridge Parkway in Pisgah National Forest. Photo by Cotter/Carol & Adrian Cotter*

the southern Appalachian mountains. In 1785 he sailed for America with his son, Francois Andre. While traveling in Western North Carolina in 1789, he discovered the prized Shartia, an evergreen plant with nodding, bell-shaped white flowers on long stalks that grew only in a limited region of the Appalachian mountains and in far-off Japan. Surely this was the American Arcadia.

Set as it was on hills overlooking the French Broad and Swannanoa rivers, Asheville's location drew dreamers and schemers alike. From Europe and the East came botanists and butterfly men such as Michaux and Lederer to explore and record the region's flora and fauna. Theirs were the first promotional tracts selling the region as the Garden of Eden. From the piedmont of the Carolinas came the Pattons, Alexanders, Davidsons, Lanes, Swains, Beards, and Vances who sought both opportunity and isolation in the mountains. Lastly, charlatans and adventurers such as Alexander Cuming and John Burton came envisioning cities and castles along the banks of the French Broad. To all of them, Asheville was a Garden of Eden in the mountains.

Top: *Asheville developed as a health resort due in part to its mountain streams. Photograph by Susan Lanier*

Above: *Lush green forests and cool waters provide an escape from summer heat. Photograph by Susan Lanier*

CHAPTER II

The Village Years

Facing page: *Hickory Nut Gap, close to the Esmeralda Inn, was one of the four traditional routes into Western North Carolina. (NCDAH)*

Asheville began as a crossroads town where the Suwali Indian trail from the east crossed another path from the north. The Suwali carried traders from Virginia as well as hostile Indians from the north into the heart of Cherokee territory. From the north came traders and settlers from Tennessee and Kentucky and the great Shenandoah Valley of Virginia. The site for the area's first courthouse and jail—sure signs of civilization on the frontier—was at the point where the two Indian paths crossed, approximately midway between the two largest settlements of Beaverdam and Swannanoa.

The present site of the new Battery Park Hotel then was called simply "River Hill." Dominating the broad valley below, River Hill rose more than 100 feet above its present height. Pack Square was also considerably higher than at present. The downhill slope toward Patton Avenue was so pronounced that early town dwellers referred to the junction of Patton and Lexington as "the dip." Because it actually was a drainage ditch, Lexington Avenue was known as "Water Street." Large rocks nearby became stepping stones to clamber up Patton, and logs were stockpiled on Lexington to help wagons up to the courthouse that dominated "Public Square." Actually a rounded hilltop, Pack Square then fell away in all directions. A ridge descended toward Lexington Avenue, reaching its lowest point at the dip, rising gradually to Haywood Street, and then shooting up abruptly to the dominating prominence of River Hill.

Rain posed a serious problem for Asheville's earliest residents. Water from River Hill found its way down to a low-lying marshy bog overgrown with water lilies and swarming with ducks and bullfrogs. Today, the frog pond is called Pritchard Park. An early resident, James M. Smith, ran a wooden culvert under the low-lying marsh to drain water into the deep ravine known today as Coxe Avenue.

Asheville owed its birth and early growth to real estate speculators such as John Burton and William Davidson and to boomers and sooners such as James M. Smith and the Baird brothers, Zebulon and Bedant. Often called Asheville's founding father, John Burton is little remembered today. A pioneer town planner, real estate broker, and grain dealer, Burton projected a town even before grants were issued. In 1793 he laid out forty-two one-half acre lots, each lying on both sides of a street thirty-three feet wide running from William Davidson's cabin and store on what is today Pack Square to the river below. That street eventually

Facing page, top, far left: *This man feeds cane into a grinder to make sorghum, circa 1914. Courtesy, W.A. Barnhill, North Carolina Collection, Pack Memorial Library*

Facing page, top, left: *Mountain streams and rivers furnished most of the power for mills throughout the region. Courtesy, W.A. Barnhill, North Carolina Collection, Pack Memorial Library*

Facing page, bottom: *One of the earliest routes into Western North Carolina was along the Swannanoa River at Connelly's Ford. This man crosses the river circa 1900. (NCDAH)*

became Main Street, today Biltmore and Broadway avenues, and, for over a century, Asheville remained largely a one-street town.

As a new county seat, Asheville was a focal point for government, mercantile, and social activities. During court week in the spring and fall, mountaineers gathered to trade goods and gossip, barter corn and pork for salt, coffee, sugar, and hardware, and drink liquor and dip snuff. Covered wagons swarmed around the courthouse and the local square became a community fair. Within a few years Asheville attracted so many mountaineers for court meeting that the county court decided to institutionalize the affair. In July 1797 Buncombe County established two fairs each year, one for the first Thursday and Friday in June, the other on the first Thursday and Friday in November.

A sharp-eyed speculator, Burton realized the importance of county business, and, in cooperation with William Davidson, conspired to have the new town become the permanent county seat. Along with David Vance, Davidson in 1791 presented a petition asking that part of Burke County and part of Rutherford County be made into a new county. The original name of the county was to be "Union," but since both Vance and Davidson fought with Edward Buncombe at the battle of Germantown, Union was crossed out and Buncombe inserted to honor the Tyrrell County hero.

Buncombe became a county on January 14, 1792. So enormous was the territory of the new county, stretching as it did westward to Tennessee and southward to South Carolina and Georgia, that for decades it was referred to as the "State of Buncombe." On April 16, 1792, the first county court met at another William Davidson's house at Gum Spring. So large and clamorous was the crowd that the first order of the new court was designed to make rowdy mountaineers respect the law. Firing into the air, Davidson ordered them to remove their coonskin hats and to be quiet. That first day the court selected officers: a sheriff, surveyor, coroner, and land entry officer, and on the next day, ordered taxes laid for 1792. Thus did civility and order come to Western North Carolina.

The court could not agree on the location of the new county seat. Asked to mediate the dispute, William Morrison of Burke County cast his vote for Burton's site near River Hill. He was rewarded by having the town named for him, and in 1794 Morristown became the county seat of Buncombe. In 1795 the name was changed to Asheville to honor the new governor, Samuel Ashe of New Hanover County, thus insuring the town's permanence and also its favor with powerful eastern politicians downstate.

Although John Burton is repeatedly noted as Asheville's founder, perhaps a better case can be made for William Davidson. One of several Davidsons to settle in Western North Carolina after the Revolution, William owned the original tract of 643 acres that became, in large part, the early town of Asheville. It was William Davidson who built the first store and log courthouse on Public Square, who sold Main Street to John Burton, who encouraged the Vance brothers to settle near him, who, in 1791, convinced his cousin (the William Davidson of Gum Spring) to introduce the bill to declare Buncombe a county, and who, according to tradition, swayed William Morrison's vote for the town site by getting him drunk in his store on the square. A promoter and politician, Davidson was no transient like Burton who moved from one scheme to another. Asheville and Buncombe County were Davidson's ideas, and he spent his life and fortune making both a reality.

Asheville soon became a focal point for speculators and adventurers. The two Baird brothers, Zebulon and Bedant, arrived in 1793 with two wagons and enough supplies to open a second store on North Main Street. James Patton offered meals and lodging to travelers in his home, the first of countless boardinghouses to be opened in Asheville. Silas McDowell tailored clothes for judges and lawyers, while George Swain made their hats in his small house and shop. With the money he made selling lots, John Burton built a gristmill on North Main Street. Always an adventurer, Burton sold his mill within months and moved to Hickory Nut Gap. There he opened a tavern, hoping to prosper on the new stage road to Charlotte and the Southwest.

On a bitterly cold day in January 1795, John Brown, a land speculator representing several wealthy Philadelphia families, rode into Asheville. Unimpressed by the "few cabins" along Main Street and the "thin settlements" throughout the region, Brown nonetheless recommended Western North Carolina as a profitable investment for his backers. Three men—David Allison, William Cathcart, and Tench Coxe, all of Philadelphia—followed Brown's advice and bought into western counties. The largest speculator in mountainland was a South Carolinian, John Gray Blount, a prominent Beaufort plantation owner and merchant. Blount owned more than one-half million acres in a vast tract bounded by Swannanoa Gap on the south and including North Buncombe, parts of Yancey, and all of Madison counties on the north. Blount's brother, William, was the governor of the new Tennessee territory, and it was their shared dream to build a road from East Tennessee through Western North Carolina. Blount envisioned a "main street of South Carolina" running from Charleston to Saluda Gap, thence to the new town of Asheville.

The first paths through the mountains were narrow but well-traveled Indian trails. Widened to crude roads by the first settlers, they became thoroughfares for traders and stock drovers from north and west of Asheville. As early as 1795, cattle, horses, mules, turkeys, and hogs produced in Kentucky and Tennessee were driven through the French Broad valley of Western North Carolina. By 1800 droving began in earnest with the construction of a new road from Greenville, Tennessee, to

Greenville, South Carolina. Only the Buncombe portion of the turnpike needed completion.

In 1824 the North Carolina legislature supported construction of an improved road through Buncombe County. Completed in 1828, the Buncombe Turnpike forever changed Western North Carolina history.

Droving increased after the construction of the turnpike. Cattle drives in November and December were the heaviest, and hogs gradually grew in numbers until they dominated the turnpike. In the 1840s an almost continuous stream of hogs moved down the French Broad River each fall. Hogs, turkeys, and cattle seem to have been driven to market the same way. Since the animals could only be driven a few miles each day, numerous stock stands and inns sprang up at intervals along the way.

The stands began approximately four to five miles from Asheville and ran in a north-south axis paralleling the Buncombe Turnpike. South of town drovers encountered Forster's Inn, Fletcher Tavern, the McDowell Hotel, Farmer's Hotel, and Colonel W.S. Tabor's place. The turnpike north of the city featured Alexander's Inn, Vance Inn, William Barnett's stand, Barnard Inn, and Patton's place near the Tennessee line. Connecting Asheville to the broad valley to the west near Murphy was Smather's while, to the east, Joseph Reed and Sherrill's Inn provided stops for weary drovers and travelers.

Occupying up to fourteen acres and consisting of lots, barns, corn cribs, sleeping halls, and large commodious boardinghouses, Alexander's Inn provided food, rest, and relaxation for drovers. At Alexander's each drove was "lotted" to itself and "corned" by the wagonload. As each wagon was driven through the lot, ten to twelve men scattered corn to the right, left, and rear of the wagon until the ground was covered. Sold at an average of fifty cents per bushel to the innkeeper, corn became the mountaineer's money crop.

Drovers were furnished large rooms with immense log fireplaces and one or two blankets. Fed sausage and ham, large biscuits dipped in gravy, fat, honey, or butter, boiled beans and cabbage, and infrequently, baked apples, potatoes, and pies, drovers ate all they could hold. Washed down by "cracked" corn, homemade cider, applejack, and steaming black coffee, meals were usually followed by "smokes" and the swapping of stories. As they retired for the night, their feet to the fire, the men formed a semicircle on the bare floor. Drovers could "eat without coaxing and sleep without rocking."

The coming of the turnpike shifted the region's economy to corn and livestock. New land was cleared to grow corn and raise stock. Innkeepers ran small stores on the side where farmers could purchase goods by barter or on credit. Not surprisingly, boardinghouses in Asheville became hotels and small stores grew to become "groceries and confectionaries." James M. Alexander opened Alexander's Hotel in 1816 on South Main Street, now Biltmore Avenue, and featured venison, wild turkey, mountain trout, and applejack as staple fare.

On the east side of South Main Street, between Sycamore and Eagle streets, Irishman William James Blair constructed a two-story frame house with a livery stable in the rear. Made famous by its mountain eagle mounted on a long slender iron staff, the Eagle became the largest and best known of Asheville's early hotels. Not to be outdone, James Smith, anxious to move from his boggy ground west of the square, soon built the Buck Hotel on the southeast side of Public Square.

The occupations of early Ashevillians mirrored the town's growth as a transportation and government center. Almost all business was conducted on what was then called "Court Square." By 1842 four attorneys practiced law in Asheville: Nicolas W. and John W. Woodfin, Joshua Roberts, and George W. Candler. Joshua Roberts founded *The Highland Messenger* in 1840, the first newspaper west of the Blue Ridge, and with the Reverend D.R. McAnally, reported on court cases and local and regional news. A tireless promoter of the region, Roberts often pleaded in his columns for "good mechanics" to settle in Asheville. "The want of Mechanics," Roberts maintained, had retarded "the growth of the village .... No village within the range of our acquaintance presents more inducements ... to settle. Almost any sort of mechanic who is industrious and attentive to business, would do well here."

By mechanics Roberts meant coopers, wheelwrights, blacksmiths, tinners, cabinetmakers, tailors, tanners, and livery stable employees. By 1845 Asheville had over sixteen shops featuring the "mechanical trades." Still, an ever-growing volume of traffic on the turnpike meant a perpetual need for more skilled workers. Stone and brick masons were in such short supply that few imposing buildings or stores were constructed before 1845. In 1846 only the courthouse, Buck Hotel, one or two brick homes on Main Street, and the newly built female academy of present-day Pritchard Park were made of brick.

In 1840 only 600 people lived in and around Asheville. Two hundred forty were slaves. Between North Main Street, now Broadway, and Beaverdam Road, the present-day Merrimon Avenue, there were only two large frame homes, an abandoned tannery, a livery stable, and an old log schoolhouse. In the middle of the approximately 400 acres bounded by North Main Street and Beaverdam Road lay an overgrown cornfield known as "old gallows field." It was here that in 1835 two horse thieves, Sneed and Henry, were hanged. Protesting their innocence to the last, both men maintained that they won the horse fairly from a card dealer at the Buck Hotel in a local game called "Old Sledge." James Smathers, the card dealer, attended the hanging and afterward rode away on his reclaimed horse.

The old Woolsey place stood perched upon a rise approximately two miles north on Beaverdam Road. Because the low-lying area below the

Facing page, top, right: *Eliza Grace McDowell was the wife of Nicholas Washington Woodfin. A lawyer and large landowner in the Asheville area, Nicholas Woodfin was honored when the community of Woodfin north of Asheville and Woodfin Street in downtown Asheville were named for him. Courtesy, North Carolina Collection, Pack Memorial Library*

Facing page, top, far right: *Corn has been a mainstay of the mountaineers of Western North Carolina since the 1820s. Hauling corn on a sled circa 1914 are (left to right) Woodrow, Esia, and Herbert Smith. Courtesy, W.A. Barnhill, North Carolina Collection, Pack Memorial Library*

Facing page, bottom: *A monument was erected on Mt. Mitchell in memory of Dr. Elisha Mitchell, who fell to his death in 1857 while climbing the mountain that now bears his name. He wanted to prove Mt. Mitchell to be the highest peak east of the Rockies. (NCDAH)*

Woolsey house accumulated water from a small stream and two adjacent springs, locals referred to it as the "Woolsey Dip." The dip, actually a wet, syrupy bog, was the main obstacle for travel on Beaverdam Road north of Asheville.

In 1840 the section of town within the triangle formed by the west side of South Main Street and Patton Avenue extending to the ravine below contained eleven homes, two stores, two stables, one tannery, and a barn. Most of the property belonged to Smith, Patton, Chunn, and James M. Alexander. The Methodist and Presbyterian churches also owned extensive property to the west of South Main Street.

From the Eagle north to the public square on Main Street stood Patton's store, a two-story brick building housing T.C. Lester's apothecary shop, and James B. Mears' mercantile house. Located next to Mears' store adjacent to the square was one of early Asheville's most famous establishments, the Drake Jarrett place, or, to local mountaineers, "Madam Swell's House." For over twenty-five years a shortlegged Frenchman known as "Monsieur" and his buxom bouncing little wife, "Madame," dealt cards, liquor, and "meretricious traffic" for drovers and mountaineers. William Morrison, a Presbyterian minister, condemned the Jarrett house as a place that "biteth like a serpent and stingeth like an adder." Confessing to Morrison that he sinned by indulging in "Mrs. Warren's profession" at Jarrett's, a local mountaineer maintained that the smiling Frenchwoman "made it right hard to resist" especially when he was "dry and forlorn."

On a wooded knoll just south of South Main Street, the Whigs, a political party opposed to Andrew Jackson's reelection, held a great barbecue in the fall of 1840. Rallying against "King Andy" Jackson and the Democrats, the Whigs dominated the politics of Western North Carolina and of the state as a whole in the two decades prior to the Civil War. Indeed, it was within early Whiggery, the concept of opposition to entrenched interests, that Asheville and Western North Carolina produced its greatest politicians—David Lowry Swain, Thomas L. Clingman, and Zebulon Baird Vance.

Western North Carolinians naturally flocked to the Whig party. Roads and turnpikes were desperately needed in the mountains. If Jackson vetoed bills for internal improvements, as he did in 1832, then Western North Carolinians voted against him and his party. If the President defeated acts to turn the federal surplus over to the states for education and improvement projects, then mountaineers, wanting schools and roads, rallied against him. Still, Whigs in frontier counties from Buncombe in North Carolina to Ashland in Kentucky were different from their counterparts in the Northeast. In their attempts to reform state constitutions, bring education to the backwoods, and to improve transportation systems, Whigs from Western North Carolina and elsewhere promoted a loose construction of the Constitution that fostered a

Above: *Born on July 27, 1812, in Huntsville, North Carolina, Thomas Lanier Clingman was one of Western North Carolina's greatest politicians. A graduate of the University of North Carolina in 1832, Clingman practiced law in Asheville, represented Buncombe County in the North Carolina State Senate in 1840, and served in the United States Congress before and after the Civil War. He also served as a general in the Confederate Army. The highest peak in the Smokies is named for Clingman. (NCDAH)*

Facing page, top: *Zebulon Baird Vance was born at Vanceville in north Buncombe County in 1830. Educated at the University of North Carolina, he was elected to Congress in 1856, where he served until 1861. When North Carolina seceded, Vance resigned to serve as colonel of the "Rough and Ready Guards" in the Confederate Army. He served three terms as governor of North Carolina and was elected United States senator in 1879, a position he held until his death in 1894. Courtesy, North Carolina Collection, Pack Memorial Library*

Above: *David L. Swain, nicknamed "Old Bunk" by his students at the University of North Carolina at Chapel Hill, was the first native lawyer of Buncombe County. Born in 1801, Swain served as judge of North Carolina Superior Court from 1830 until 1832. He was governor of North Carolina for three successive terms and president of the university for thirty-three years. (NCDAH)*

new national spirit. Nowhere was the newly aroused passion for democracy more keenly felt than in Asheville and Buncombe County.

After 1835 party conventions—a new form of democratic electioneering—were held in Raleigh. Equally important, Whig and Democratic organizations sprang up in Buncombe County in support of the state convention. Political rallies usually occurred in the fall during court week. From farms, huts, and cabins, mountainmen streamed into Asheville, their wagons filled with food and drink. The fences along Court Square became crowded with boisterous mountaineers who drank and debated political issues of the day.

The great barbecue of 1840 featured small containers shaped like log cabins filled with whiskey and open wagons crowded with musicians who traveled slowly up and down Main Street and around Court Square. Mountaineers wore coon skins and keg caps, sang "Tippecanoe and Tyler too," drank hard cider, fired their weapons into the air, and shouted at everyone to "jump on the bandwagon." In 1840 Democrats were "too scarcely to count."

Vance, Clingman, and Swain remembered the riotous mass meetings in Asheville as the yeast-time of their careers. "Them was POLITICS!" Vance swore. To survive, politicians had to possess an organ-like voice, a keen wit to counter the jibes from the audience, and a mighty roundhouse punch to flatten the opposition. Vance once recalled that at a meeting there were "fifteen separate and distinct fights . . ., in part of which I participated and for all of which I might be set down as the proximate cause."

The Highland Messenger shamelessly promoted the Whig cause in Western North Carolina. A Methodist minister as well as a firm believer in the Whig cause, Reverend D.R. McAnally, one of the paper's founders, doggedly tried to inspire local mountaineers to a higher morality. "Quarreling, fighting, stabbing, shooting, wounding, and killing have become so common," McAnally complained, "that we do not pretend to keep up with the accounts." Before progress and advancement came to Asheville, he asserted, the people themselves must improve their "manners and morals." Doomed to disappointment, McAnally eventually left Asheville.

CHAPTER III

The Battle of Asheville

Facing page: *Confederate veterans were welcomed on July 4, 1889, at the residence of General J.M. Ray. The Ray home at Woolsey was located at the present intersection of Mount Claire and Hillside streets. General Ray is at the extreme left, Mrs. Ray is seated, and Captain Weaver is on the extreme right. Courtesy, North Carolina Collection, Pack Memorial Library*

The Civil War came to Western North Carolina in April 1861. Still a mountain village, Asheville's population had grown to over 1,000. The chief buildings lay scattered on Main Street beginning with the first bend south of the square on the Greenville stage road and extending northward to Nicholas Woodfin's house. Still boxing the square on the north and south, the Buck and Eagle hotels had a new rival, the Carolina House. The Carolina House catered not to drovers and herders but to an increasing number of seasonal tourists from South Carolina. North and south of the square, businessmen such as Rankin and Pulliam, E.O. Aston, Hugh Johnston, Jessie Smith, Patton and Summey, B.H. Merrimon, and a number of smaller merchants operated stores in substantial brick buildings along Main Street. The Bank of Cape Fear, the town's first, was located just south of the square on the west side of Main Street while the county's first brick courthouse dominated the square. Together with two-score scattered homes, four churches, and two schools, this formed the village of Asheville in 1861.

Still, Asheville, the "Queen City of the Mountains," as Zebulon Vance dubbed her, was destined to become a military center for the Confederacy during the next four years. Ashevillians and their neighbors in Buncombe County were almost alone in the mountains in their support of the Confederate cause. While other mountain towns and counties were torn by conflicting loyalties to the North and South, Asheville and Buncombe were not. Indeed, Senator Andrew Johnson of Tennessee referred to Asheville as "That damned secession hole in the mountains," and, from Zeb Vance to Stephen Lee, the city and county fought on long after Robert E. Lee had surrendered at Appomattox.

At the beginning of the war a young Zebulon Vance proposed that Asheville be named the capital of the new Confederacy. Citing its central location, attractive climate, and relative isolation, Vance claimed it would be an ideal site. Never taken seriously in the first years of the war, the idea of Asheville as a last Confederate capital reemerged in the spring of 1865 as a dying Confederacy looked to the mountains as a last redoubt.

In not-so-far-away Virginia in late March 1865, Lee's last remaining army fought off an overpowering Federal force under Grant, retreating south and west after evacuating Petersburg and Richmond on April 2. Farther south, Joseph E. Johnston's army stubbornly resisted the relentless advance of Sherman's troops as they moved into North Carolina.

In the first week of April 1865 both southern armies might have been able to join forces for one last stand in the mountains of Western North Carolina. To forestall such a possibility, Union forces planned three invasions of Western North Carolina in the spring of 1865.

By March 1862, Asheville had become a small but growing Confederate military post. Troops from throughout the region trained at Camp Patton, located at the present intersection of Charlotte and Chestnut streets, and at Camp Jeter near the junction of Cherry and Flint streets in Montford. In the center of town a Confederate commissary acted as a distribution point for clothing and foodstuffs shipped to North Carolina regiments throughout the South. Nearby, Dr. James F.E. Hardy, a local physician, operated a military hospital. Throughout the war, he functioned as a one-man medical staff, operating on and treating hundreds of Confederate casualties. Public Square became a convalescent center for soldiers recovering from illnesses and wounds.

When this picture was taken in 1866, Colonel "Zeb" Vance was returning to private law practice after two terms as wartime governor of North Carolina. In 1876 he was again elected governor, and in 1879 United States senator. (NCDAH)

The fortifications of the town were few but effectively located. To the east, cannon and earthworks were erected on Beaucatcher Mountain. Two positions in Asheville—one consisting of trenches on the north side of Woodfin Street and another of breastworks on the site of Highland Hospital—were fortified. Two Napoleon guns were dragged to the highest point in town, River Hill, now called Stony Hill, and designated Battery Porter after its commander. About a mile and a half north of the city earthworks were thrown up at "Dead Man's Curve" on the Buncombe turnpike. It was here that the Battle of Asheville was fought on April 6, 1865.

By far the most important Confederate establishment in Asheville was an armory. Located at the northeast corner of Valley and Eagle streets and run by Captain Benjamin Sloan, it furnished thousands of Enfield rifles to the South during the war. At first Sloan had found the work almost impossible, but he kept going. Without a steady supply of coal for the forge, Sloan burnt charcoal. A black pall of smoke hung over Eagle and Valley streets. By the spring of 1863, over "300 beautiful and efficient muzzle loading rifles were turned out monthly." The armory's success made it the target of raids from "organized bands of disaffected mountaineers on the lower French Broad River, who were encouraged and backed by . . . disaffected citizens of East Tennessee." It was Sloan who planned the fortifications in and around Asheville and who, with Stephen Lee, organized a home guard to defend the town against marauding bands as well as from a Union attack. Called the Silver Greys, the home guard had in it older men, young boys, disabled veterans, and convalescing soldiers. The youngest was James Hardy Lee, thirteen, whose father commanded the Greys, the oldest a Baptist minister of seventy. A roll call in May 1864 contained forty-four names.

By late 1862 Asheville had become the assembly point for training soldiers in the southern mountains. One of the companies equipped at

The Zebulon Vance Camp of Confederate Veterans was the largest in North Carolina and regularly met in Asheville. This particular meeting, in front of the Nicholas Woodfin home, took place in October 1927. Courtesy, North Carolina Collection, Pack Memorial Library

Camp Patton came from Henderson County. Called the "Edney Greys" after their commander, B.M. Edney, the Greys were notable for their "great physical stature." As Lawrence Pulliam, an older resident, later recalled, the Edney Greys "made a grand appearance in dress parade. Their color bearer was a man named Brock, and I remember him as one of the tallest men I have ever seen."

Zebulon B. Vance organized a company from Asheville and Buncombe County known as the "Rough and Ready Guards." Never at a loss as to what to do or say, Vance characterized his troops as "awfully rough but scarcely ready." In 1862 he became North Carolina's war governor.

James M. Gudger eventually succeeded Zeb Vance as commanding officer of Company F, the "Rough and Readys." Wounded twice, Gudger still "held on to his boys until the war was fought out." At the battle of Chancellorsville on May 3, 1863, Company F, "100 strong, left the streets of our beautiful little village to meet the enemy." Every member of the "Rough and Readys" was either killed or wounded during the war. Only twenty-four survived.

The regular army troops of the Western District of North Carolina were commanded by James Green Martin. While serving in the Mexican War in 1846, Martin's right arm had been torn off by grapeshot. Thereafter his troops fondly called him "Old One Wing." Initially placed in charge of all state forces, Martin trained, armed, and sent to war more than 100,000 North Carolina troops. After his health began to fail in the winter of 1864-1865, Martin was sent to Asheville to recover. There he commanded troops in the Western Mountain District. In March 1865, Martin had less than 2,000 troops to defend Western North Carolina from an anticipated Union invasion.

The Union army in Tennessee prepared a three-pronged sweep into Western North Carolina. From Newport, Tennessee, Colonel George Kirk crossed the Smokies into Haywood County near Maggie Valley. Colonel Isaac Kirby then followed the old Buncombe Turnpike along the French Broad River toward Asheville. Farther east, General George Stoneman, employing Sherman's scorched-earth tactics, entered Watagua County on March 26.

A native Tennessean, Kirk had "a well-earned reputation as a desperate and brutal character." Kirk's force included few regular Union army troops. Composed mainly of Confederate deserters, local bushwhackers, and Union sympathizers, they had no temper for pitched battle, especially so late in the war.

At Cataloochee Kirk was met by Confederate Colonel James R. Love with a company from the Sixty-ninth Regiment. Avoiding the determined Confederates, Kirk moved further west to Soco Gap in the Balsam Mountains. There, Lieutenant James Conley ambushed Kirk's men, driving them to Soco Creek where a combined force from Jackson and Swain counties together with Cherokee Indian Confederate soldiers awaited them. Surprised by the fervor of the opposition and afraid of more ambushes deep in Cherokee territory, Kirk hastily retreated across the Smokies along the old Thomas Road toward Sevierville. Shielded by Love and his Confederates in the west, Asheville, for the moment, was safe from Union raiders.

The greatest threat came straight down the Buncombe Turnpike. On April 3, 1865, Colonel Isaac M. Kirby of the 101st Ohio Infantry left his camp at Greenville, Tennessee, to "scout in the direction of Asheville." At Asheville Kirby expected to link up with Kirk and Stoneman. Starting early on the morning of April 3, Kirby had with him over 900 infantry, two cannon, a train of over seventy wagons, and supplies for seven days. More than seventy Confederate deserters and Union sympathizers from Western North Carolina who knew the terrain rode with him into Madison County.

From the beginning, Kirby seems to have been intimidated by the imposing mountains ahead. He believed that the mountains of Western North Carolina were the highest east of the Mississippi, a fact not at all reassuring to an Ohio flatlander like Kirby. Moreover, Confederate deserters convinced him that mountaineers shot at anyone in uniform, whether blue or grey.

Keeping close by the French Broad, Kirby nervously anticipated attack from all directions. Convinced that Colonel William Thomas' feared Cherokee legion was on the other side of the river, Kirby burnt every bridge between Warm Springs and Asheville. Apprehensive that bushwhackers would shoot his horses and prevent his return to Tennessee, Kirby stole every animal he could find enroute.

Disorganized by rumors of Yankees everywhere, Confederates in Asheville were not prepared to meet Kirby's advance from the north. Nicholas Woodfin, too old for combat in 1865 but still a warm-hearted secessionist, first recognized Kirby's scouts. Overseeing his farm in what is now part of north Asheville, Woodfin spotted Kirby's men and rode into Asheville at full gallop, firing his weapons to sound the alarm. Summoning troops from nearby Camp Jeter, Colonel George Wesley Clayton hastily assembled and marched a company for the Sixty-second Regiment along North Main Street, now Broadway, to the fortifications opposite Glenn's Creek. Confederate trenches and breastworks ran along the ridge just north and east of the creek.

By noon Clayton's men had been joined by the Silver Greys, some Confederate regulars home on leave, a local fire company, two constables, and several dozen well-armed citizens. Two cannons, hurriedly moved from Battery Porter hill, strengthened the Confederates' positions.

The battle began at three o'clock in the afternoon of April 6 and ended just after dusk. Although over 1,000 men and several cannons were involved in more than five hours of combat, no one was killed. For their part, the Federals had no desire to press the attack. Kirby's orders decreed that he scout in the direction of Asheville, not engage in decisive battle or try to take the town. Lacking artillery, having only cursory intelligence on the enemy's strength, running low on provisions and munitions, commanding unreliable and poorly trained troops, and operating deep in southern territory, Kirby did not desire a pitched battle. Instead, he retreated.

Clayton similarly had little reason to press the issue. Outnumbered and with few regular troops at his command, his mission was to defend the town, not pursue retreating raiders. Furthermore, Clayton had scanty stores of shot, shell, lead, and powder to fight a sustained battle. Instead his men engaged in a running, desultory firefight with the Federals. A drenching late afternoon thunderstorm aided the Confederate effort not a little. Clayton was content to hold his position and wait for an assault.

One danger still remained. In December 1864, General George Stoneman struck northeastern Tennessee and southwestern Virginia, ripping up railroads and destroying Confederate supplies to prevent Lee's retreat into the mountains. After destroying the Confederate prison at Salisbury and cutting the Greensboro railroad line to Danville, Virginia, Stoneman turned westward, leaving what one historian described as "a trail of loot, riot, pillage, and murder" in his wake. By April 17 only Asheville remained as the last major Confederate sanctuary in Western North Carolina.

After taking Morganton, Stoneman detached General A.C. Gillem and his troops to take Asheville. In Asheville General Martin unofficially heard of Lee's surrender from returning Confederate soldiers. Other veterans confirmed the report, and by April 21, Martin realized the war had ended. With Federal troops now within six miles of town, Martin, under a flag of truce, asked to negotiate with Gillem. On April 24, the two met at Busbee's place on Hendersonville Road to work out a temporary peace. The next day Federal troops entered Asheville. That evening Gillem and his staff dined with Martin while Gillem's men, camped just outside the town, were provisioned from Confederate stores. At sunrise the next morning the Federal troops left Asheville heading north into Tennessee.

Then disaster struck. Discontented with being kept out of the town and convinced that Asheville was not punished enough, some of Gillem's raiders under General Brown wheeled about and reentered Asheville at dusk on the evening of April 26. Composed of three regiments—one black and two of Confederate deserters and Union sympathizers from Western North Carolina and Tennessee—Brown's men sacked the town. Just home from Virginia, Colonel James M. Ray was awakened by sounds of gunfire and shouts near the square. "Before I had gone a hundred yards toward town," he recalled, "three cavalrymen came dashing around the corner opposite Woodbury's stable, firing their pistols recklessly and shouting and yelling." Ray hid in the woods near Beaucatcher Mountain. From Beaucatcher "an appalling sound reached our ears . . . . It was the sound of a soldierly mob gutting houses of whites and negroes alike, ripping open beds, tearing away ceilings, weatherboarding and plaster in search of hidden treasures. They made the night hideous with their yells."

In the next few weeks hundreds of refugees, paroled Confederate soldiers, and freed slaves passed through Asheville. Realizing they were free and could locate where they chose, blacks in Asheville migrated almost en masse toward Tennessee. Some few moved to Henderson County where they joined freedmen from the lower south to form a utopian community called "The Kingdom of the Happy Land."

On May 13, Zeb Vance's birthday, a squad of Confederate cavalrymen rode into Asheville, chased around the square shouting "Hurrah for the Southern Confederacy," fired their weapons into the air, and sprinted out of town as quickly as they came. It was the last hurrah for the South's lost cause in Western North Carolina.

Facing page, top, right: *Major John W. Woodfin wrote his will in the form of a letter to his brother after having a premonition concerning his death. He was killed during a skirmish at Hot Springs during the Civil War. Courtesy, North Carolina Collection, Pack Memorial Library*

Facing page, top, far right: *Confederate veteran Dave Penland made bark buckets in the 1900s. Courtesy, W.A. Barnhill, North Carolina Collection, Pack Memorial Library*

Facing page, bottom: *General Thomas L. Clingman (first row, second from right) attended the Rebel Reunion at Waynesville on August 28, 1889. The assembly was made up of veterans from the Richland Rifles and the Rough and Ready Guards. Others who attended the reunion were Governor D.G. Fowle (front row between women), Judges A.C. Avery and J.E. Shepherd, General R.B. Vance, Colonel J.S. McElroy, Honorable T.D. Johnston, and other statesmen. Courtesy, North Carolina Collection, Pack Memorial Library*

CHAPTER IV

Victorian Asheville

Facing page: *In this typical scene of Victorian Asheville, a woman and her daughter gather flowers in the Woodfin section. Courtesy, J.H. Tarbell, North Carolina Collection, Pack Memorial Library*

In 1876 a young woman named Christian Reid published a maudlin love story about Asheville called the *Land of the Sky.* Coinciding with the rediscovery of Appalachia as a different kind of South after the Civil War, Reid's book painted an idyllic picture of Asheville and of Western North Carolina as a Garden of Eden whose inhabitants were caught in a curious time warp. The mountaineers of Western North Carolina in the post-Civil War era were viewed as "contemporary ancestors," remnants of a hardy race descended from pioneer forefathers who continued to live in frontier days. Lacking adequate transportation, Asheville and Western North Carolina had been isolated from the rest of the state and nation for so long that it appeared to outsiders as a region fundamentally different from the rest of the South. It was a separate land, the "land of the sky."

When the Western North Carolina Railroad finally reached Asheville on October 3, 1880, its promotional literature described the town and surrounding mountains in Reid's terms as the "land of the sky." The first of a long series of pamphlets and brochures selling Asheville and the mountains, Reid's work was aimed at tourists, at invalids from the piedmont, and at the summer people who saw in the town a "Saratoga of the South," a Victorian town set in the Garden of Eden.

In the book Reid anticipated the three ingredients essential to an ambitious town in Victorian America: a railroad, a large mill, and an elaborate hotel. The railroad should have reached Asheville before the Civil War. In 1855, Zeb Vance introduced a French Broad railroad bill into the state assembly. The 1855 act became the authority which finally brought the railroad to the mountains. Work on the line frequently lapsed because of insecure funding. By 1861 the Western North Carolina Railroad had reached Connelly Springs just east of Morganton. There work stopped until after the war.

The drive for a railroad to Asheville and Western North Carolina intensified after the Civil War. Between 1871 and 1879 attempts and schemes to build a railroad to Asheville were so numerous that the state failed to appropriate funds to maintain existing stage roads and turnpikes. Infuriated because "railroad schemers" neglected the turnpike, Buncombe County commissioners in July 1871 presented the Western Division of the Western North Carolina Railroad Company a bill to pay for the "bad condition of the . . . Turnpike."

The failure to bring the railroad to Western North Carolina in the

Facing page, top, far left: *This early resident of Asheville poses for a portrait in 1897. Courtesy, J.H. Tarbell, North Carolina Collection, Pack Memorial Library*

Facing page, top, left: *A young mountain boy sits in front of his cabin located in Chunn's Cove in 1909. Chunn's Cove acquired its name from Samuel Chunn who was granted land on both sides of Sunset Mountain. Chunn served as chairman of the Buncombe County Court, as jailer, and as commissioner of Asheville. (NCDAH)*

Facing page, bottom, far left: *A convict work gang composed mostly of blacks repairs a roadbed on the railroad near Asheville. Blacks furnished the majority of the labor for the railroads around the Asheville area. Many black section hands brought their banjos with them, an instrument which was introduced to America by the blacks. (NCDAH)*

Facing page, bottom, left: *Fiddling and banjo playing became a favorite pastime of mountaineers at the turn of the century. Musicians and dancers provided local color for tourists and outsiders. Courtesy, W.A. Barnhill, North Carolina Collection, Pack Memorial Library*

decade after the Civil War and the continued deterioration of existing roads meant that Asheville, after the prosperity and growth of the drover's era, was relatively more isolated in 1875 than it had been fifty years earlier.

In 1875 two major obstacles prevented the extension of railroad lines into Western North Carolina. The first involved the problem of "the gap at Swannanoa," tunneling and grading through the mountains; the latter the tangled finances and speculative schemes of railroad companies. For a decade after the Civil War both seemed insurmountable.

Nineteenth-century railroad companies were wildly speculative and experimental in their tactics and schemes. The province of politicians and stockjobbers, early railroad companies in North Carolina seldom laid a mile of track, preferring instead to buy and sell stocks in expectation of a quick profit. Actual construction of lines frequently was in inverse proportion to poorly laid plans.

An early visionary scheme called for the establishment of a great port at Wilmington with a system of railroads running through Salisbury, Charlotte, and Asheville on through Murphy to Ducktown. Gauges would be different from those in South Carolina and Virginia so that the state's commerce would stay within its own borders. Work on the route to Asheville stopped altogether in 1871 when state officials found that George Simpson and Milton Littlefield, Western Carolina Railroad's two highest ranking officials, had made off with all the company's funds. Work resumed in 1879 when the state sold its interest in the road to William Best, James Fish, J. Nelson Tappan, and William Grace on condition they finish the line by July 1, 1881. Only "the gap" stood in their way.

The completion of the line west to Asheville languished in the slow progress of the tunnel through the Blue Ridge at Swannanoa Gap. Adopted as the best method of crossing the mountains, the Swannanoa tunnel challenged late nineteeth-century technology. While workers on the eastern side of the tunnel labored with steam shovels, drills, and locomotives, those on the western end had only picks, shovels, and oxen to assault the mountain. For years little or no work was attempted on the western side of the tunnel. The long and costly haul of the debris by wagon down the mountain effectively slowed and eventually halted work in the west.

It was left to Ephraim Clayton, a Confederate veteran, to solve the problem of tunneling from the west. Hired to complete the work, Clayton, surveying the site in 1879, calmly asserted that "men move mountains." To overcome the predicament of hauling tons of rubble away from the construction site, Clayton proposed laying a temporary track and winching a steam locomotive over the mountain to do the work. Given enough men, oxen, and time, it could be done. State officials sent gangs of convicts to help in the work, and Clayton hired hundreds of mountaineers with

Facing page, top, far left: *After the railroad opened Western North Carolina to tourists in the 1880s, mountaineers increasingly sold their crafts and wares at shops and hotels in Asheville. Courtesy, W.A. Barnhill, North Carolina Collection, Pack Memorial Library*

Facing page, top, left: *Carding wool is a painstaking step in weaving. Courtesy, W.A. Barnhill, North Carolina Collection, Pack Memorial Library*

Facing page, center: *With the influx of tourists and visitors to the Asheville area, the city became the center for the sale of southern crafts. Local mountaineers, such as this couple making apple butter in a brass kettle, brought their handmade goods into the city for sale. (NCDAH)*

Facing page, bottom, far left: *Sulphur Springs was discovered in February 1827 by Robert Henry. Three years later Henry's son-in-law, Colonel Reuben Deaver, built a wooden hotel on the site. From 1889 through 1894 an electric railway ran from Asheville to the springs, which were located five miles west of Asheville, now Malvern Hills. Courtesy, North Carolina Collection, Pack Memorial Library*

Facing page, bottom, left: *Built between Old Fort Mountain and Asheville, the Round Knob Hotel was a stopping point for the railroad which connected the mountains of Western North Carolina to the piedmont. Andrews Geyser was an added attraction. (NCDAH)*

their oxen to help out. At times the locomotive moved only inches each day. Still, the engine together with its plucky engineer, an old Scotsman named Nelson Aldrich, was placed on its western tracks in less than a month. The completion of the line to Asheville was assured.

To get through the tunnel, Clayton hired a friend and fellow Confederate veteran, Thad Coleman, master builder of the Carolinas, to help with construction. Skilled in the use of nitroglycerine and an avowed perfectionist, Coleman personally placed charges of blasting powder and jugs of nitroglycerine throughout crosscuts in the mountain. Although the road from Ivy down the French Broad, where explosives were hauled, was destroyed and several people killed by infrequent explosions, Coleman boasted that no one was ever injured by his blasting. When the tunnel was finished on March 11, 1879, he strode to the east-west dividing point, connected the telegraph line, and wired Asheville that "grades and centers met exactly." On hand for the ceremony, James W. Wilson of the Western Carolina Railroad proudly proclaimed that "daylight entered Buncombe County today through the Swannanoa tunnel." The first train from Salisbury arrived at Best Station, now Biltmore, on October 2, 1880. A new era had begun.

The coming of the railroad to Asheville and Western North Carolina forever changed the region. Lured by promotions touting Asheville as an untouched village in the "land of the sky," outsiders flocked to the mountains. Tourists from the east and southeast, invalids from the sultry piedmont of the South, capitalists, speculators, adventurers, and summer people from all over came to the new "Saratoga of the South" to resort, to recreate themselves, and above all, to make money.

Until 1880 Asheville was only a rural county seat, a crossroads village with hogs running wild in the streets and wagons loaded with corn and wood mired in the mud around Pack Square. So slowly did the town recover from the devastation of the Civil War that by 1868 it had only six stores, a post office, four taverns, and less than 1,200 inhabitants. Described as a "pretty country town in 1870," a visitor remarked that the chief occupation seemed to be "the manufacture of illicit corn whiskey" and its open sale on Court Square. Indeed, it took a century for Asheville's population to grow from a score of people to 1,500 by 1870. In the decade from 1880 to 1890, Asheville became a city with more than 10,240 residents.

The Eagle Hotel dominated social life in 1881. "There is a gay, glittering, smiling, surging crowd of visitors at the famous Eagle Hotel," a visitor remarked. "They are laughing, talking, dancing, flirting, as they do at summer resorts everywhere." Everything seemed extravagant and romantic. Visitors' accounts of Asheville in the 1880s described the town in idyllic, even poetic terms. "Oh Asheville," gushed one Raleigh matron, "Behold the scene! Drink deeply in the beauty and the grandeur of the surrounding country and your very senses will be steeped in

intoxication. As far as the eye can reach you behold the everlasting mountains . . . . The city of Asheville lies like a dream at your feet." While Asheville and the mountains were looked upon as a second Garden of Eden, local natives were Lil'Abners and Daisy Maes. The town was inhabited by "big-boned, semi-barbaric people . . . picturesque with groups of motley, grizzled, and long-haired men in slate-covered homespun." Although the Eagle and Swannanoa hotels became a social refuge for the summer people, primitive mountaineers nonetheless were everywhere. They added an element of local color to a visit. "One is apt to stumble across some odd characters at places of this kind," Mrs. Whitson, a Raleigh visitor, asserted.

Asheville's four bars clustered around the square. X Brand and Company, a curious firm located on North Main Street, served as an undertaking establishment and an overnight resting place for drunks and vagrants. Farther down Patton Avenue near Haywood Street, a boardinghouse, "The Misses Coffin," operated as yet another local entertainment center.

Arriving in 1887, visitor A.W. Long observed that the bars were "none too clean inside and loafers around the front doors do not add to the attractiveness of the Square." Horses and mountaineers drank at the public pump and at several watering troughs around the square. The combination of mud, men, oxen, horses, and hogs made Court Square seem less a convivial gathering place and, to Long, more like "a public cesspool." Visitors generally stayed away from the square, especially at night.

As mayor three times during the crucial decade when the railroad came to Asheville, Edward J. Aston determined not only to promote the city as a health resort but also to clean up Court Square. Under Aston, a new courthouse was completed in 1877 at a cost of $33,000. Remarkably, it had a third-story opera house with a seating capacity of over 400. Across from the new courthouse the old public stocks and whipping post were torn down and replaced by benches and a public water

Above, left: *The railroad came to a stop west of Salisbury. The Civil War, economics, and the Blue Ridge Mountains prevented the railroad from coming to Asheville until 1880. Courtesy, Ewart Ball Collection, Southern Highlands, UNC-Asheville*

Above: *Farm machinery was slow to come to the mountains of Western North Carolina. These men are thrashing rye along the Blue Ridge during August 1912. (NCDAH)*

Facing page, right: *The Swannanoa Hotel opened its doors for business in 1880, the year the railroad came to Asheville. Named after the famous Swannanoa tunnel, it was located on South Main Street (now Biltmore Avenue). The hotel also housed a clothing store called Bon Marche run by Solomon Lipinsky. Courtesy, Ewart Ball Collection, Southern Highlands, UNC-Asheville*

Facing page, far right: *Asheville's leisurely elegance is expressed in this 1890 portrait. Courtesy, J.H. Tarbell, North Carolina Collection, Pack Memorial Library*

Above: *Mountaineers traditionally brought wood into Asheville to sell to the town dwellers for construction and heating. The wood market, photographed here circa 1883, was located next to Pack Square. (NCDAH)*

pump. Aston donated over 200 books from his personal collection to start a circulating library. He insisted that the square be called "Court Square" and not Public Square, hoping that the new name would give it more dignity. Lastly, Aston dreamed of paving the streets around the square, a project that later was completed under Mayor Blanton in 1893.

In 1881 Asheville still lacked a stately hotel worthy of the Victorian era. The Eagle and Swannanoa were not suitable. "It is a stupid idea," Mrs. Whitson insisted, "building a hotel for summer visitors in the midst of the business portion of the city. People like to get away from those things." A picturesque and romantic setting was required. Mrs. Whitson instinctively felt drawn to the wooded area atop Battery Porter, the old Confederate redoubt. The views there were "absolutely enchanting. If some enterprising company would build a handsome hotel, and furnish [it] with all the modern improvements, it doubtless would become the most popular resort in the city. Imagine a few fountains, several hundred rustic seats, croquet grounds . . ., no one could want anything nicer."

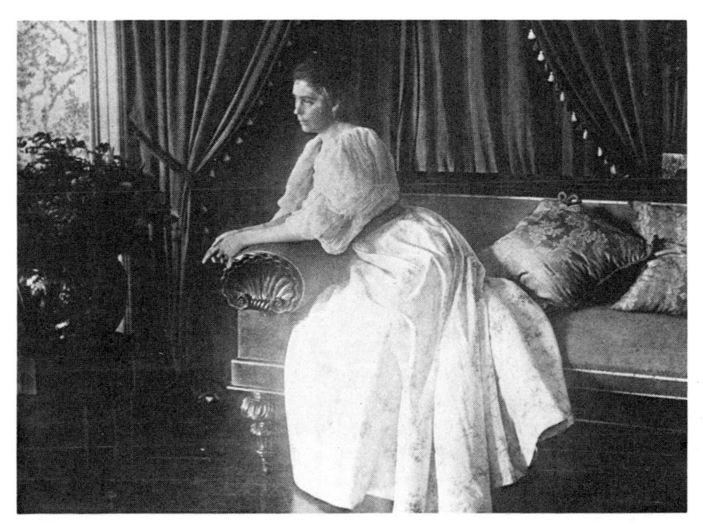

CHAPTER V

The Castle Builders

Facing page: *George Washington Vanderbilt purchased 125,000 acres in the mountains of Western North Carolina in the mid-1880s. Under the architectural supervision of Richard Morris Hunt, Vanderbilt began the construction of his 250-room estate in the summer of 1890. With the help of hundreds of workmen and artisans from all over the country, the Biltmore House opened five years later. Courtesy, Biltmore House and Gardens Archives*

The railroad not only brought tourists and summer people to Asheville, but capitalists and entrepreneurs as well. From Philadelphia via nearby Rutherford County came Frank Coxe, from St. Louis, Edwin W. Grove of pharmaceutical fame, and from New York City, George Washington Vanderbilt, a member of one of America's best-known families.

Financiers and moneyed men, gentlemen and tastemakers, the Coxes and Groves came not only to enjoy the refreshing scenery and exhilarating climate, but also to make money. E.W. Grove became the designer of modern Asheville, always striving to change the city from a tourist and resort center to a convention and business hub. A railroad promoter and founder of the magnificent Battery Park Hotel, Coxe soon epitomized Victorian Asheville and its railroad era. With his estate and castle south of town, Vanderbilt focused national attention on Asheville and on all of Western North Carolina.

Two of the castle builders reputedly carved out their fiefdoms in a turn-of-the-century conversation at the old Battery Park Hotel that likely never took place. In a gentleman's agreement aimed at preventing cutthroat competition, Vanderbilt and Grove supposedly agreed on a division of Asheville and Buncombe County between them. Grove took the area north of the city and developed hotels, resorts, and neighborhoods northward to the present-day Beaver Lake. Vanderbilt located his Tudor village and magnificent Biltmore house and estate just south of Asheville. Frank Coxe developed the downtown area around old Battery Porter hill. All three built castles that came to symbolize the dreams that each had for Asheville and its future.

Franklin Coxe grew up at Green River plantation in Rutherford County near Spindale. When the railroad reached Asheville, Coxe, a part owner of the Western North Carolina line, turned his attention toward perhaps his greatest enterprise, the Battery Park Hotel.

Designed in Philadelphia and built in Asheville by John A. Wagner, the Battery Park Hotel symbolized Victorian Asheville. The very name of the hotel, pleasant and patriotic as it was, gave it a distinction beyond the Plazas and Ritzes. It was here that Confederate guns had been placed to hold off the Yankees and where young boys had come to play.

Coxe intended for the hotel to be located at the center of a beautifully landscaped Victorian park. An easy ascent now, Battery Park's steep grade presented a problem to builder John Wagner in 1885. He located the entrance to the driveway near present-day Haywood and

Above: *President William McKinley, in the top hat, visits the old Battery Park Hotel in 1897. Courtesy, J.H. Tarbell Collection, Pack Memorial Library*

Above: *In a very rare photo, George W. Vanderbilt holds his only daughter, Cornelia, on the veranda of his estate in Biltmore. Courtesy, Biltmore House and Gardens Archives*

Above: *Colonel Frank Coxe, proprietor of the old Battery Park Hotel, arranged stagecoach rides for his visitors. Known as the "Tallyho" group, visitors enjoyed romantic rides up to Beaucatcher Mountain and other scenic spots. Courtesy, Mrs. Trench Coxe*

Facing page, top: *A couple of tourists enjoy a beautiful trout fishing hole during the summer of 1911. Asheville's major hotels organized fishing and sightseeing expeditions of the surrounding mountains and streams for their guests. (NCDAH)*

Wall streets and, by using switchbacks and cuts, made the ten-minute ride up the hill an inviting excursion among flowers, trees, fountains, gazebos, croquet fields, and lawn chairs and tables.

Opened on July 12, 1886, the old Battery Park Hotel was one of the finest resorts ever built in Western North Carolina. Each room had its own fireplace, modern steam radiator, and, a new innovation in 1886, Edison electric light bulbs. Under the dining room, billiard and bar rooms and smokers catered to "gentlemanly pleasures." Yet the hotel was remarkably liberal for Victorian America. Men and women mingled freely for the first time, a modern touch, and there were no side entrances to the ladies' parlor or to the gentleman's billiard room.

The Victorian age was a time that demanded more starched linen in a gentleman's suit, more ruffles and lace on ladies' gowns, more verandas on hotels and rocking chairs on porches, more courses on menus, and more affectations in manners and conduct. Parties, socials, clubs, the theater, walks in the park, and brisk carriage rides to Mount Mitchell or Mount Pisgah—all the heady social scene of Victorian Asheville seemed to descend from the magnificent hotel atop the old battery hill.

Prominent families in the area began to hold socials at the Battery Park. Numbers of balls and receptions were held each year, gala assemblies that attracted throngs from everywhere. Gradually, the events became seasonal—a rhododendron ball in August, an anniversary dance in July, the famous German party to greet the fall, and a Christmas hop. The first anniversary party, held on July 12, 1887, set the tone for future affairs.

The anniversary party began on a Saturday evening at ten o'clock. Thousands of Chinese lanterns shed long lines of red, green, and blue light upon the carriages stopping at the *porte cochere.* Over 1,200 guests attended, crowding the grand piazzas and gathering in the spacious ballroom to hear the orchestra open with the grand march. Flowers, ferns, and palms decorated the ballroom while "the rich colors of bunting of each of the flags of the southern states" graced the dining room.

The lavish setting only provided a backdrop for "the toilettes of the ladies," many of which "excelled in richness of material and elegance of design." One of the "most perfect toilettes" of the evening belonged to Mrs. A.J. Lyman, "a court train of heavy [layers] of heliotrope satin over a petticoat of pansy velvet, ornaments, diamonds, pearls, and a garniture of duchesse lace." The evening began with champagne punch served at specially erected tents and ended with "Tipsy Pudding"—a mixture of milk, eggs, and cornstarch laced with whiskey—served at daybreak. Too drunk to stand, two party guests, both prominent city leaders, were hauled in wagons to Church Street at sunrise where they delivered fiery sermons on temperance to their congregations.

The hotel's menu improved with the arrival of E.P. McKissick as manager. Friendly and outgoing, McKissick determined to make the Battery Park's cuisine the equal of its social events. To do this, he combined European and local dishes. Thus, he offered elaborate meals featuring pineapple pigeon, Simla chicken from the East, and Rococco cream from Europe as dessert. His opossum dinners on Thursdays and mountain trout dinners on Sundays became staple events.

The old Battery Park Hotel dominated Victorian Asheville. Almost every photo or painting during the period showed the hotel towering over the city with its stately sky tower and elegantly landscaped park. Purchased by Dr. Edwin W. Grove in 1921 for the development of the hill for business purposes, the old hotel was finally demolished in 1924.

George Washington Vanderbilt came to Asheville in December 1887, and stayed at the Battery Park Hotel. A scholar who spoke eight languages and who read and traveled widely, he chose Richard Morris Hunt to build "the greatest castle in America." Already famous as the first American to graduate from the Ecole of Beaux Arts in Paris and as a designer of the World Exposition at Chicago, Hunt gave Vanderbilt the French chateau he wanted.

Built in the French Renaissance style of the mid-sixteenth century, Vanderbilt's estate was patterned after three castles in the Loire valley of France. To complement Hunt's work, Vanderbilt chose Frederick Law Olmsted, perhaps America's greatest landscape architect, to sculpt the estate's grounds.

Weakened by old age and embittered by the failure of his past projects, Olmsted saw in the Biltmore project a chance to complete his "greatest work of art." A social democrat who believed that land, if

Facing page, top: *Frederick Law Olmsted was commissioned by Vanderbilt to do the elaborate landscaping that surrounds the Vanderbilt estate. (NCDAH)*

Facing page, bottom: *A fire department was formed to protect the Biltmore Forest community. Established as a separate township in 1923, Biltmore Forest became an exclusive residential area for wealthy retirees. Courtesy, Ewart Ball Collection, Southern Highlands, UNC-Asheville*

Biltmore Forest

Facing page, top, far left: *All Souls Episcopal Church, with its brick turrets and steeply pitched roofs of clay tiles, was designed in the early Gothic style by Richard Morris Hunt. Built in the 1890s by George W. Vanderbilt, All Souls is the center of Biltmore Village. (NCDAH)*

Facing page, top, left: *Built in eleven months and twenty-seven days from boulders taken from Sunset Mountain and the surrounding area, the Grove Park Inn was the dream of Edwin Wiley Grove from Paris, Tennessee. Grove employed Italian stonemasons and hundreds of local laborers to construct the 500-foot-long granite and steel structure. Courtesy, Grove Park Inn*

Facing page, bottom: *Large numbers of blacks came to Asheville from 1880 through 1920 to work in the rapidly increasing tourist and resort industry. A group of employees pose in front of the Grove Park Inn, circa 1920. Courtesy, Ewart Ball Collection, Southern Highlands, UNC-Asheville*

used harmoniously with the urban environment, could do much to relieve the social ills of overcrowding and despoilment, Olmsted designed some of America's most magnificent parks. The problem, Olmsted maintained, was a simple one, that of *trompe l'oeil.* Parks and landscapes must be designed in pastoral settings so natural and beautiful that the eye of the beholder would be fooled. The landscaping of the Biltmore House would be Olmsted's lasting achievement. The house forever would be safe from urban encroachments, protected by an approach road that would prepare visitors by exposing them to three miles of carefully laid-out scenes.

A pharmacist by trade, Edwin Wiley Grove began his career in Paris, Tennessee, in 1874. Constantly experimenting with drugs and chemicals, Grove wanted "to render quinine, the wonder drug, tasteless" so that it would have popular usage. By 1891 sales of his tonic annually totaled more than one-half-million dollars. In 1957 Grove Laboratories was purchased by the Bristol-Myers Company which still continues to produce several of Grove's original products.

A summer resident, Grove moved to Asheville because of his wife's health. After starting a chemical plant on South Main Street "to keep his hand in," Grove turned to real estate. Fascinated by the idea of building a unique resort overlooking the city, he began buying up acreage on Sunset Mountain. Constructed in eleven months and twenty-seven days, Grove Park Inn opened on July 1, 1913, with William Jennings Bryan delivering the official address.

The inn did little to satisfy Grove's speculative temper. He went on to purchase land in Georgia, Florida, Tennessee, and North Carolina, to develop properties in Atlanta and Swannanoa, to buy the old Battery Park Hill area from the Coxes, and to envision a new downtown for Asheville. In 1922 Grove announced his three-point plan to revitalize downtown Asheville. He intended "to provide Asheville with a tourist center featuring a large roof garden, with band shell, restaurant and assembly room," to build an arcade where a large number of business establishments could be housed, and "to preserve the beauty of the Battery Park district by uniform and pleasing architectural treatment of the plaza." The new Battery Park Hotel and the Grove Arcade across from it were the first steps in Grove's grand scheme for downtown Asheville. Grove died in 1927 before his plans were finalized.

Why did business leaders from New York, Philadelphia, and St. Louis build castles with spectacular views, libraries, billiard rooms, several dining rooms, art galleries, and even small theatres? In the get-rich-quick business mentality of Victorian America, castles such as the Grove Park Inn, Battery Park Hotel, and Biltmore House demonstrated the wealth of their builders. The castles were visible bank accounts. Local mountaineers said that Grove Park Inn cost over two million dollars to build when the actual cost was only about $175,000. If the purpose was visi-

Above: *This carving shop was included in the Biltmore Industries begun by Edith Vanderbilt. The carvings on the wall are typical of the ornamentation found around the estate. Courtesy, Biltmore House and Gardens Archives*

Facing page, top: *Fred Seely, E.W. Grove's son-in-law, frequently invited his friends to spend the summer in Asheville. Pictured in front of the Grove Park Inn in 1918 are Seely and a few of his guests (left to right): Harvey Firestone, Sr., Thomas Edison, Harvey Firestone, Jr., E.W. Grove, Henry Ford, and Seely. Courtesy, Ewart Ball Collection, Southern Highlands, UNC-Asheville*

Facing page, bottom: *Opening in 1899, The Manor Inn had twenty-five rooms and was part of a park designed and built by William Green Raoul of Savannah. Raoul, often faced with the problem of finding accommodations suitable for his large family, included fourteen cottages on the grounds, each of which could house twelve people plus servants. Courtesy, Ewart Ball Collection, Southern Highlands, UNC-Asheville*

bility and display, imprecision such as this was always an added advantage. The absence of an income tax, or much taxation at all, added to the attractiveness of the investment.

Since all the castles employed labor, their construction and maintenance created work and jobs. All three men supported the arts and helped local charities. Their castles adorned and beautified Western North Carolina, and, indeed, became objects of local pride.

Still, not everyone admired the region's castle builders. Grove Park Inn was described by an Ashevillian as "a delirium of the stone cutter," and a bitter mountaineer condemned the Battery Park Hotel for refusing to admit him because he was "too shaggy." Some residents resented the black section hands and Italian immigrants brought in to work for the castle builders. James Wainwright, a resident of south Buncombe, perhaps summed up the general suspicion of a great many mountaineers. "Millionaires must cost us something," Wainwright asserted, and he was sure that somehow he would wind up helping to pay for "Mr. Vanderbilt's big house."

CHAPTER VI

Blacks in Asheville

Facing page: *This little girl attended the Mountain Street School in 1900. The school was renamed the Lucy Herring School in 1965. Courtesy, North Carolina Collection, Pack Memorial Library*

The first blacks came to Western North Carolina with the Indian traders who made the long journey overland from Virginia, Charleston, and Augusta. When Cherokees came to East Flat Rock in the 1730s, blacks were with them both as slaves and as free men. Samuel Davidson, the first white settler, had slaves on his farm, as did many settlers. Still there were few blacks in the mountains until the 1830s.

Blacks came to the mountains in three waves—the 1830s, 1880s, and in the two decades after the turn of the century. They were brought by the opening of the great Buncombe toll road, by the coming of the railroad in the 1880s, and by the burgeoning resort and tourist industry of Thomas Wolfe's Asheville. Blacks in large numbers came from the areas around Orangeburg, South Carolina, Salisbury, North Carolina, and Knoxville, Tennessee.

Before the Civil War education for blacks in Western North Carolina was clandestine at best, usually little more than infrequent meetings in fields, homes, and cellars. With the end of the Civil War blacks looked to education as the key to entering society as free and equal participants.

The coming of the railroad in 1881 brought large numbers of black section workers and laborers to the mountains. With them the demand for public education grew. Although private schools had sprung up among churches and missionary societies after the Civil War, there were still no public schools for blacks by 1880. In 1887, Isaac Dickson, son of a slave mother and a Dutch father, was appointed to the Asheville city school board. Vigorously campaigning for public schools for blacks, Dickson helped organize the first school for blacks in an abandoned building on Beaumont Street. The school opened in 1888 with three teachers and over 300 students in the first five grades. Over 800 were turned away. Paid $25 a month—less than half the salary of a white teacher—Beaumont Street's teachers concentrated on basic literacy. Dickson helped establish Catholic Hill school in 1891, the first public high school for blacks, and, within the next three decades, Hill Street, Livingston Street, Mountain Street, and Burton Street schools would all be built. Black public schools were all constructed before 1922 and it would be thirty more years before they would be renovated or rebuilt.

Founded in 1887 by the Women's Home Missionary Society of the Methodist Church, Allen School became a model of its kind. Begun as an elementary school, Allen extended its status as a high school for black women in 1924. Built on land near Beaucatcher Mountain donated by the L.M. Peases of New York City, Allen first held classes in an abandoned livery barn. Named for Marraige Allen of London, who donated money for the main dormitory built in 1897, the school combined a rigorous program of classical and vocational education. So successful were its graduates that Allen soon attracted students from all over the Southeast.

Catholic Hill School burnt down in 1917 in one of the greatest tragedies ever to strike Asheville's schools. Seven students were killed, several others seriously injured. In its ashes rose Stephens-Lee, perhaps the best known of black schools. Named for Hester Lee, the deceased wife of principal Walter Smith Lee, and educator Edward Stephens, the new high school mirrored the philosophy of W.S. Lee, certainly the dominant figure in black education after Isaac Dickson, Educated at Livingstone College and at Columbia University in New York, an enthusiastic follower of Booker T. Washington, Lee emphasized a curriculum built around dignity, self-help, and Shakespeare. At Stephens-Lee, that meant courses in carpentry, radio repair, welding, home economics, cosmetology, English literature, music, and drama.

Stephens-Lee became a center for black culture and education throughout the mountains. When Yancey County's secondary school for blacks burnt down, students were loaded into a small, unheated bus and driven to Stephens-Lee. Blacks from Yancey County daily made a four-and-a-half-hour drive into Asheville. With the only other black high school in the area in Hendersonville, a great many black mountaineers from surrounding counties found their way to Stephens-Lee.

Stephens-Lee quickly became known for its classical music program, drama production, and in the 1930s, its marching band. Only in the last decade of Stephens-Lee's existence did competitive athletics play a major part in the school's history. Coaches such as Oliver W. McCorkle and Clarence Moore always emphasized community programs and athletics as recreation, never as a system to promote the gifted few. Stephens-Lee enhanced the spirit as well as the intellect of black mountaineers. Plays, band concerts, and basketball games all drew large crowds.

In an era when blacks were denied access to most public facilities, schools substituted as neighborhood centers. Schoolyards became outdoor gyms and playgrounds, daycare centers, meeting places for church and civic groups, centers for adult education, public libraries, and places where music and entertainment were available. Only the Young Men's Institute and black churches had similar, if limited, resources for the community as a whole.

The crisis over integration in the early 1960s and the subsequent decision to close Stephens-Lee challenged the very traditions of blacks in Western North Carolina. To them, Stephens-Lee was more than just a school. Representing the two strongest elements of black mountain-

Facing page, top, right: *Isaac Dickson helped organize the first school for blacks in Asheville. In 1887 he was appointed to the Asheville City School Board. Courtesy, Ewart Ball Collection, Southern Highlands, UNC-Asheville*

Facing page, top, far right: *These children pose in Asheville circa 1897. Courtesy, J.H. Tarbell, North Carolina Collection, Pack Memorial Library*

Facing page, bottom: *Many black women worked as nannies in well-to-do white homes. Courtesy, North Carolina Collection, Pack Memorial Library*

eers—community and education—Stephens-Lee stood as a symbol of black achievement, independence, and culture. The hill where the school was built had been the center of black education for over a century. It was there that the first "arbor school" for slaves had been built, where the first school for blacks was organized after the Civil War, where the only black high school known by many mountaineers had been for over sixty years. More than any issue during the integration crisis of 1962-1972, the decision to close Stephens-Lee and move blacks to South French Broad divided white and black mountaineers.

From their beginnings in the 1830s until today, churches for black mountaineers have remained "a rock in a weary land." Almost all share the same origins they came into existence from Free African churches begun before the Civil War, from Southern Protestant branches, and from northern missionary efforts in the 1880s.

Nazareth First Baptist Church, for example, had its origins among slaves who came to the mountains in the 1830s. Nazareth's congregation began in 1862 as a Sunday School class taught by slave-owner Tom Patton's daughter. After the Civil War, a log cabin was built on Pine Street on land donated by Patton. In 1867 the members named the church Nazareth.

Established in 1880 by Robert Rumley, Mt. Zion Missionary Baptist Church first held meetings in an upstairs room of Henderson Hall. A charismatic leader and speaker, Rumley became a vital force in Mt. Zion's early history. Black and white mountaineers came from miles around to hear him speak.

Organized in 1915, Hill Street Baptist Church long associated itself with community affairs. Hill Street early organized a daycare center and recreation program for Ashevillians.

An Episcopal congregation arose in 1868 when black members of Central Methodist Church, protesting discrimination in the church, withdrew to form a "temple of worship for the Negro race." Angry at having Sunday School classes outside at the back of the church building and at the Methodists' refusal to let a black minister address them, blacks instead met under a brush arbor near Beaucatcher Mountain. Led by Reverend Hopkins, the group rented a schoolhouse on Clemmons and Pine streets until their own church was completed. Renaming the church Hopkins Chapel, the congregation affiliated itself with the AME movement, perhaps one of the oldest independent black denominations in America.

Second Lieutenant James Bryant Dickson was one of the first black men from Asheville commissioned as an officer in the U.S. Army during World War I. James was the grandson of Isaac Dickson, the "father of black Asheville," for whom Dickson Street (now Eagle and Valley streets) was named. Courtesy, Ewart Ball Collection, Southern Highlands, UNC-Asheville

Hopkins Chapel produced one of Asheville's best-known sons, the Bishop W.J. Walls. Known as the "Boy Minister" of Hopkins Chapel, he vowed to take the "Hopkins message" throughout the nation. Educated at Livingstone College in Salisbury and at the University of Chicago where he worked with Bertrand Russell, Walls exhibited great organizational skills. His successes included founding the largest black church in Louisville, Kentucky, and also helping to organize Roosevelt University after World War II. In the 1960s Walls became part of the international ecumenical movement, bringing his message of cooperation, dignity, and self-respect—the "Hopkins message"—to a worldwide audience. Camp Dorothy Walls in Black Mountain, founded by Walls and named for his wife, and Heritage Hall at Livingstone College, dedicated to the preservation of "the heritage and culture of black people everywhere and to foster international studies," are both eloquent tributes to Bishop Walls and his work.

Of all the black churches in the mountains, St. Matthias Episcopal Church retains its early links to the Vanderbilts. Unable to allow freedmen to worship at All Souls and eager for blacks to undergo "the episcopal experience," Vanderbilt donated materials and craftsmen from his estate to build St. Matthias in 1895. Indeed, the beautiful ceiling and scrollwork of St. Matthias' interior rival that of the Biltmore House.

At least two other church notables stand out in Asheville's history. Under the direction of Charles B. Dusenbury, Calvary Presbyterian Church was organized in 1881. Sponsored by the northern Freedmen's Board, Dusenbury sought to establish "a soap and water gospel" among mountain blacks. Dusenbury began by preaching in the old Catholic Hill church, and, in 1884, setting up a parochial school in the basement. Enrollment quickly reached 150. Dusenbury's school emphasized basic literacy and a few skills such as hygiene and gardening. Charles Dusenbury died in 1920; his school closed in 1927.

Dr. Charles A. Edington became pastor of Calvary Presbyterian in 1934. No less interested in "enlightenment and uplift" than Dusenbury, Edington associated himself with community affairs ranging from Boy Scouts to businesses, from the YMI to the NAACP. Known as the "Pastor

Lucy S. Herring, pioneer black educator in Western North Carolina, taught for fifty-two years in the Asheville area. Mountain Street School was renamed the Lucy Herring School in her honor. Courtesy, Ewart Ball Collection, Southern Highlands, UNC-Asheville

of Eagle Street," Edington concerned himself with the affairs of black mountaineers for over a quarter of a century.

For over eighty years the Young Men's Institute has been both the heart and soul of Asheville's black community. Constructed by George W. Vanderbilt in 1892-1893 as a community center, the YMI was intended to serve not only Asheville's blacks but also the hundreds of laborers involved in the construction of Biltmore, and blacks throughout Western North Carolina. The original idea for the YMI came from Edward Stephens, a native of the West Indies who was educated at Cambridge University in England. Brought to Asheville by Vanderbilt, Stephens quickly realized that there were few public facilities for blacks throughout the region.

Land for the YMI was purchased for a small sum from Martha Patton, long a supporter of the black community. Built by Richard Sharp Smith, supervising architect of the Biltmore House and perhaps Asheville's best known architect, the YMI bears a noticeable resemblance to buildings in Biltmore Village and estate and throughout the city.

The YMI succeeded even past Stephens' imaginings. Throughout much of the present century the building housed shops, residence and meeting rooms, a drugstore, real estate firm, undertaker, cabinet shop, city library, beauty shop, barber and shoe shop, and offices for physicians, dentists, lawyers, and druggists. Churches, schools, and civic clubs met at the YMI. In the magnificent auditorium people banqueted, danced, listened to concerts and songfests, and played basketball. In the basement, they boxed and wrestled on dirt-covered floors.

The YMI has been rescued from oblivion not once but three times in its history. The first came in 1906 when forty-nine of the most prominent black leaders in Asheville pledged $10,000 to buy the building from the Vanderbilts. In 1944 Dr. Robert M. Hendrick led a reorganization and renovation which, in 1946, culminated in the YMI's becoming the South Market Street Branch of the YMCA. The most recent chapter of the YMI, begun by John Baxter and a group of concerned citizens, now has as its goal the return of the building to its original function as the center of Asheville's black community.

The struggle for equal rights for black mountaineers occurred in three phases. Beginning in 1887, the first clash was over public education and participation in city government. Isaac Dickson emerged as the leader and the beginning of black public schools as the result. The second skirmish began after World War II and ended with the renovation and reconstruction of schools such as Hill Street and the appointment of Western North Carolina's first black postal worker, radio announcer, and city policeman. The most recent episode came in the period from 1965 to 1972. Triggered by the decision to close Stephens-Lee and inflamed by the city's foot-dragging in hiring blacks, particularly on the police force, the last phase resulted in the full integration of Asheville

High School and of city government. To many blacks, the 1980s appear more disquieting than any decade since World War II. Faced with a racism more sophisticated and complex than in the past, confronted by unsympathetic officials in courthouses and statehouses, challenged by a new generation of blacks who know little of segregation and discrimination, and impeded by leaders and institutions organized in the 1960s to fight civil rights battles, many blacks in Asheville face the future with a tempered optimism.

When set out comprehensively, the record of black mountaineers is that of quiet determination and attainment. The lives of most black mountaineers, like those of the majority of Western North Carolinians, are dominated by hard work, family, continued struggle, and an unusual concern for community. Even so, black mountaineers have been notable achievers.

Isaac Dickson should long be remembered as the father of black education in the mountains, and Edward L. Stephens as the inspiration for community organizations such as the YMI, and for his belief in excellence in education. Albert E. Manley served as principal of Stephens-Lee in 1934. Afterward he went on to receive his Ph.D at Stanford and eventually to become president of Morehouse College in Atlanta. John H. Michael pioneered summer schools for black teachers in the mountains and ceaselessly pushed for recreational facilities for blacks until a gym was built at Hill Street in 1940. Lucy Herring was such a dominant force in promoting kindergarten and elementary education for all mountaineers that, in 1961, Mountain Street's name was changed to Lucy S. Herring School. From 1938 to 1966 Eugene Smith edited and published a version of *The Southern News,* the mountain's only black newspaper. Smith's newspaper circulated within six southern states and he remained a dominant political force in the mountains for almost three decades. Today, Henry Robinson unpretentiously carries on Smith's proud tradition by effectively reporting the news of black mountaineers with the Asheville *Citizen-Times.*

E.W. Pearson tirelessly fostered fellowship among mountain blacks for almost forty years. A promoter of agricultural fairs for blacks, Pearson gave away prizes for canned goods and crafts. It was Pearson who organized lodges and fraternal organizations for blacks, eventually extending his lodges throughout the Carolinas.

For his part, William E. Roland contributed to the integration of lunch counters, the removal of color signs from department stores, and the opening of Pack Library to everyone. Serving as president of the Asheville-Buncombe County Citizens Organization Roland helped draw up Asheville's desegregation plan. David Jones, Jr., as a member of the Housing Authority, helped develop and implement plans for timely integration of all-black and all-white neighborhoods. Reuben Dailey, Asheville's first black city councilman, represented the interests of both

Facing page, top, right: *The Young Men's Institute building housed many businesses, including this drugstore. Dr. Jones (center) and Dr. W.G. Torrence (right) were two Asheville physicians, photographed inside the drugstore in 1910. Courtesy, Ewart Ball Collection, Southern Highlands, UNC-Asheville*

Facing page, top, far right: *Founded in the 1890s to serve as an educational, social, and cultural center for blacks in Western North Carolina, the Young Men's Institute became noted for its band. Much in demand in Asheville's hotels and resorts, the YMI Band specialized in classical and jazz music. Many of the musicians pictured here went on to colleges and universities throughout the region and became well-known musicians and teachers. Courtesy, Ewart Ball Collection, Southern Highlands, UNC-Asheville*

Facing page, bottom, right: *Western North Carolina's first black little league was organized in 1957 and sponsored by the Asheville Varsity Club. Courtesy, Ewart Ball Collection, Southern Highlands, UNC-Asheville*

Facing page, bottom, far right: *Lucy S. Herring, seated at right, was honored as the Woman of the Year by Zeta Phi Beta Sorority in 1952. Ms. Herring was again honored as one of North Carolina's outstanding women of achievement in 1986. Courtesy, Ewart Ball Collection, Southern Highlands, UNC-Asheville*

white and black Ashevillians. John Baxter, Ernestine Caldwell, and Lucy Herring carefully collected and preserved the records of black mountaineers. Teachers such as Daisy Glenn devoted their evenings to teach others to read and write.

Throughout their long history, black mountaineers have banded together not only in churches but also in a wide array of community organizations. Long before the United Way came to the mountains, blacks formed the Negro Welfare Council which sponsored recreation and playground activities, music, games, drama productions, crafts, hikes, picnics, and clubs. In 1937 the Welfare Council reached out to 72,453 black mountaineers. Before blacks were admitted to physicians' offices and hospitals, the Flower and Fruit Guild visited the poor, sick, and elderly bringing baskets of food and flowers with them. It seemed natural for many black mountaineers to move into opportunity centers for senior citizens in the last two decades and to offer their skills and help there. After all, it had been a community tradition for over a century.

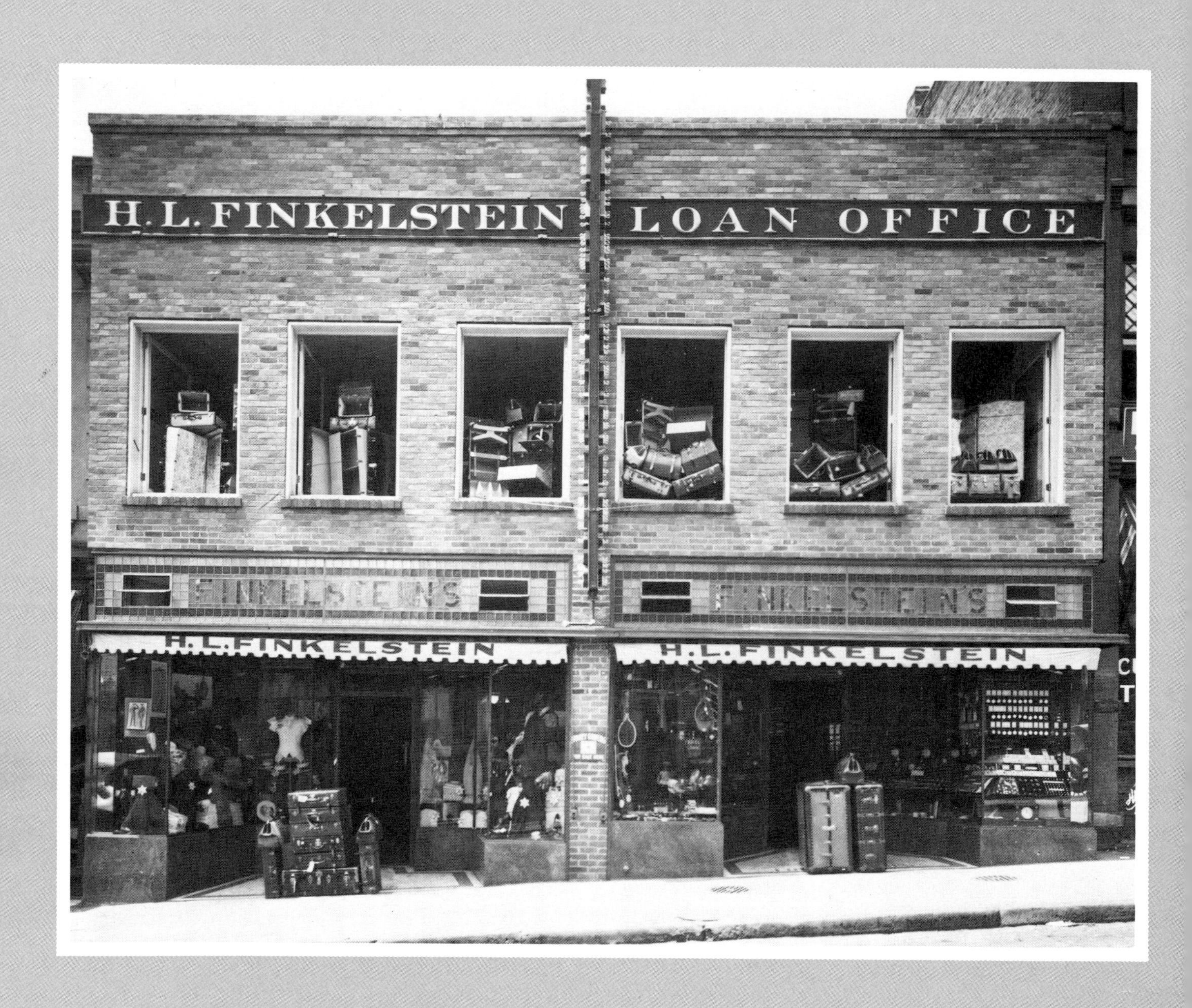
H. L. FINKELSTEIN
LOAN OFFICE
FINKELSTEIN'S
FINKELSTEIN'S
H. L. FINKELSTEIN
H. L. FINKELSTEIN

CHAPTER VII

A Coat of Many Colors

Facing page: *Known as the "poor man's bank," Finkelstein Loan Office is shown here at its first location on South Main Street circa 1930. The business operated in downtown Asheville for more than fifty years. Courtesy, Ewart Ball Collection, Southern Highlands, UNC-Asheville*

Asheville's growing popularity as a resort and health center lured outsiders to the city in the 1880s. Not only did the Coxes, Vanderbilts, Groves, and Packs come to Asheville, but also large numbers of immigrants, especially Greeks and Jews. Indeed, it was the presence of large numbers of blacks and immigrants in Asheville that, in a fundamental way, gave it a sense of otherness that set it apart from surrounding counties. As a city, Asheville wore a coat of many colors.

The Jews who came to Western North Carolina in the early decades of the nineteenth century came as peddlers. Called "egg eaters" by the Cherokee Indians because they would not eat meat of any kind until they returned to Asheville to observe the Sabbath every Friday, Jewish peddlers quickly established a reputation among the Indians for fairness and a refusal to trade in alcohol.

As a walking department store, the Jewish peddler also was welcomed by farmers and pioneers throughout the region. Carrying several hundred pounds of goods on pack horses, his wares included socks, suspenders, linens, curtains, taffetas for Sunday dresses, needles, and hardware from nails to iron skillets. For the youngster, the peddler brought geegaws and toys, for the farmer, precious news from the outside world.

Still regarded as strangers and not as residents, Jews in significant numbers settled in Asheville in the 1880s. They came partly because of the region's booming economy and, additionally, because of the influence of Zebulon Baird Vance. Having served as North Carolina's Civil War governor and then as United States Senator, Vance was known throughout the nation for his fiery independence and defense of Southern rights. By the 1880s, Vance also had emerged as a folk hero to Jews in the South. It was Vance who, in 1868, defended the right of Jews to be seated in the state legislature. Jews would be especially welcome in North Carolina.

By the late 1880s the Jewish peddler had become the merchant, and, eventually, the prince of merchandising in Western North Carolina. Solomon Lipinsky became one of many Jewish merchants who came to Asheville in the following decades and who, by their business ideas and application, forever changed the art of merchandising in the southeast. Lipinsky introduced the large single-price store into Western North Carolina where the price of each unit independently was attached to each item. Merchants Barney Pearlman, Joseph Max Cooper, Robert Zageir, and Solomon Harris Michalove followed Lipinsky, opening clothing and dry goods stores around Asheville. Butchers, bakers, and restaurateurs followed, notably the Paul family, Kubler and Whitehead, and the Schandlers.

The first Jews who came to Asheville contributed substantially to the city's economic and intellectual growth. Well-established financially and generally accepted socially, Asheville's small Jewish community had become, in the 1920s, mountaineers who saw Western North Carolina as their permanent home.

Submerged within a society that was primarily Anglo-Saxon and fundamentalist Protestant, Asheville's first Jews turned to Reform Judaism. Lacking the supporting neighborhood of a larger city, long established in Asheville as part of the community, and coming from an Ashkenazic culture that did not stress Zionism, Asheville's Jews became more relaxed in their faith, keeping the spirit more than the letter of Hebrew law.

Two subsequent waves of Jewish immigrants to Asheville tended to be more conservative. The first, coming after World War II, expressed their revulsion over the Holocaust and their support of the new Israeli state by stressing traditional rituals and observances. Another group whose background lay in ethnic neighborhoods of large northeastern cities such as New York and Boston began arriving in the 1960s.

Almost from the first, Jews who came to Asheville profoundly affected the city's cultural development. The Jewish community brought with them a high regard for education, a cosmopolitan view of the world outside Asheville, and, lastly an optimism that offset mountaineer fatalism. It was, for example, the Lipinskys and Zageirs who were instrumental in establishing a unit of the University of North Carolina system in Asheville, the Edwinns and Rosenbaums who wanted a symphony for the city, and Josef Vandewart who helped a chamber music series survive in a small urban environment.

It was in the area of social justice and civic improvement that Asheville's Jews made their greatest contributions. Many of Asheville's Jewish leaders stepped forward during the racial troubles of the 1960s trying to heal the split within the community. Many of Asheville's greatest civic projects—the Civic Center, regional airport, Memorial Mission Hospital, Red Cross, and the United Fund—either originated in or were made successful in part by the support of Asheville's Jewish community. People like Helen Gumbert, Ruth and Leon Feldman, Julius Levitch, and families such as the Lipinskys, Zageirs, Edwinns, and Rosenbaums have significantly contributed to Asheville's cultural growth.

The first Greeks settled in Asheville in the 1880s, arriving on the newly opened railroad and opening a cafe near the old riverside depot. Large groups or congregations of Greeks never came, but a steady trickle made its way to the mountains until by 1975 more than 415 Greeks made Asheville and Buncombe County their home. At present, approxi-

Facing page, top: *The Bon Marche department store, originally located in the Swannanoa Hotel, moved to a new building, pictured, at the corner of Battery Park Avenue and Haywood Street in 1923. Established by Solomon Lipinsky of Asheville, the store was operated by the Lipinsky family for more than eighty years. Courtesy, Ewart Ball Collection, Southern Highlands, UNC-Asheville*

Facing page, bottom: *Operated by the Meyers and Fortune families, the Palais Royal was one of Asheville's largest department stores before 1900. Courtesy, Ewart Ball Collection, Southern Highlands, UNC-Asheville*

PALAIS ROYAL

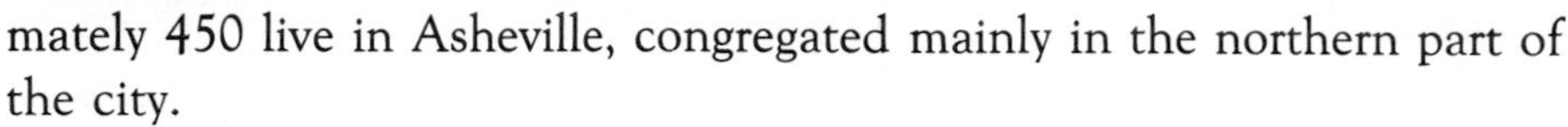
mately 450 live in Asheville, congregated mainly in the northern part of the city.

A great many early Greek immigrants worked in service jobs, peddling fruit and vegetables around Pack Square in pushcarts, operating small refreshment stands, and working in the food business. By 1923 the most typical occupation was in cafes and restaurants. "First we open a cafe," boasted Gus Peterson, a Greek immigrant of the 1920s, "then a church." By 1985 Greeks owned or managed forty-five food-related businesses in Asheville and Buncombe County.

Loosely organized and scattered, the Greek community comes together through the Orthodox Church. Until 1935 services were conducted by a circuit-riding priest at the home of Charles Chakales, one of the first Greeks to come to Asheville. As the Greek community grew they rented two floors above an old clothing store on Patton Avenue. The upper floor served as a chapel while the lower accommodated a language school for children.

As early as 1923 Greeks in Asheville established a church building fund. Several families donated funds for over forty years. In 1947 the old N.B. Morris estate on Cumberland Avenue in Montford was purchased. A debt-free church was built beside it in 1967. To Greeks the church initially symbolized solidarity in an alien country. It furnished support, community, and a link to the past. The simplest way for Greek immigrants to live in America was by working with other Greek families, almost all of whom belonged to the church. From the first, Greeks learned to help each other and to succeed through the promotion and maintenance of an Orthodox community. After Greeks were comfortably settled in an area, the church then served to pass Greek customs,

Above, left: *Edna Lichtenfel, with her husband Gustave, was one of Asheville's leading philanthropists. She helped to establish the local Red Cross and was instrumental in lining Charlotte and Kimberly streets with trees. Courtesy, Ewart Ball Collection, Southern Highlands, UNC-Asheville*

Above: *Theresa Chakales Alexander is a descendant of one of Asheville's oldest Greek families and an authority on Greek immigration to the region. Courtesy, Ewart Ball Collection, Southern Highlands, UNC-Asheville*

traditions, and the language itself on to future generations as measures of security and strength.

The Greek emphasis upon family, church, and community reinforced older mountain customs and traditions. While Greeks took their children with them to dinners and celebrations, so did native Ashevillians. If Greeks were clannish, then Western North Carolinians were, too. The Pattons, McDowells, Westalls, and Vances reflected many of the same values as did the Demos, Chakales, and Zourzoukis families. Deeply religious and church-oriented, local mountaineers admired the Greeks' sense of piety and devotion to their church. To Ashevillians, Greeks had become a vital part of the community, considerate neighbors, proficient businessmen, and, most important of all, good friends.

Thus far the history of Jews and Greeks in Asheville has been one of expectations realized, of success and accommodation to a mountain culture. In Asheville Jews and Greeks have prospered and been welcomed. Here both groups have felt free to exercise their political and religious liberties. A Greek or Jew can run for city council, serve in the state assembly, or become governor. At the same time, they freely observe their religion, sustain their traditions, and perpetuate their culture.

Gathering funds for the war effort, the ladies of the Red Cross hold a rally on Pack Square in 1918. Enough money was raised to purchase a field service ambulance in memory of Kiffin Rockwell, Asheville native son and aviation pioneer who was shot down over Europe early in World War I. Courtesy, North Carolina Collection, Pack Memorial Library

CHAPTER VIII

Asheville's Mind and Spirit

Facing page: *The first mid-year graduation class of Asheville High School in February 1908 consisted of (left to right) Carl Collins, Edwin Phillips, Paul Henry, Bettie H. Moore, and Curtis Ownbey. Courtesy, North Carolina Collection, Pack Memorial Library*

George Newton, a Presbyterian minister, was furious at the ignorance and lack of formal religion he found in the raw frontier town of Asheville in 1800. He petitioned Buncombe County for laws to restrain the "vice and depravity" all around him. Newton noted that "many gross immoralities daily abound among the citizens, of which intemperance in the use of ardent spirits, profane swearing, and breach of the Holy Sabbath are none of the least." Failing to persuade the county court, Newton took his campaign to the people.

Mounting the back of a wagon on the public square before an astonished crowd, Newton pointed a bony forefinger southward toward Swannanoa and, in a thunderous voice, declared that "there is the root of all evil." The Swannanoa settlements, Newton insisted, were filled with "ignorant Methodists, back-sliding Presbyterians, and once-dipped Baptists." What Asheville needed, Newton insisted, was "education and a right-thinking doctrine," namely, Presbyterianism. A year later Newton became master of his own academy. Ashevillians, heeding Newton's advice, banned Baptists from Church Street and managed to keep them out of town for over fifty years.

In early Asheville there were no church buildings. Denominations held services in downtown stores, in the old courthouse, at the Reverend Newton's new school, in homes, or outdoors in meadows and groves of trees.

Bishop Francis Asbury of the American Methodist Episcopal Church began to include the French Broad valley in his annual circuit. Soon Methodism had taken root in Western North Carolina. The first Methodist church in Asheville, a frame house standing at the site of the present Central Church, was erected in 1837. Curiously, Central Methodist became the mother of churches in Asheville. Trustee William Coleman went on to become a minister himself and found other congregations. His wife, Evelina Coleman, converted to the Episcopal Church and helped establish the first congregation in Asheville. Upset at the ministry at Central Methodist, Nicholas Woodfin contributed in 1859 to the establishment of "Trinity Church . . . worshipping according to the forms of the Protestant Episcopal Church." Hopkins Chapel, perhaps one of Asheville's best-known black churches, began in 1868 when black members at Central Methodist, angry at having to attend Sunday school classes at the back of the building and not inside, withdrew to form a separate congregation.

Although George Newton would have preferred to keep Baptists out of Asheville, they were there from the first. In 1789 Edward Sams raised the first Baptist church in the county, Hominy Baptist on North Hominy Creek. Well-educated Presbyterian and Methodist ministers such as Newton and John Dickson constantly decried the Baptists' "want of knowledge" and "howling, unenlightened services."

Largely because of the efforts of Thomas Stradley, Baptists slowly began to take root in Asheville. An Englishman with a "qu'ar voice" and "steady eyes," Stradley impressed James Alexander as a "high-type Baptist fellow." When Stradley came to Asheville in the summer of 1830 he found Baptists meeting in a ramshackle log structure. The father of Asheville's Baptists, Stradley remained for forty-five years, pastoring the congregation as it moved from place to place. In 1927 First Baptist moved to a new, magnificent brick church, designed by Douglas Ellington, where they have since remained.

In October 1842 James Patton and Samuel Chunn gave part of their land just off North Main Street and Patton Avenue for a Presbyterian church. Together, the Chunns, Pattons, Moores, Hawkins, and Whitesides joined to form a new congregation. For the next seventy years First Presbyterian remained the most important and dominant church in Asheville. John Dickson, a well-educated congregationalist preacher, became the Presbyterian's first regular minister.

Although small in numbers, Catholics were present in Asheville and Buncombe County from the beginning. Several French Catholics lived in Asheville before the Civil War, frequently meeting for informal services in W.D. Rankin's home. In 1869 Rankin conveyed to James Gibbons land on a slope that came to be known as Catholic Hill. Five years later a brick structure was completed, and liturgical services begun. In 1889 the congregation moved to the end of Haywood to accommodate Catholics from the North who stayed at the Battery Park Hotel.

In 1907 Rafael Guastavino, an internationally acclaimed engineer and architect, designed the church of St. Lawrence, one of the architectural masterpieces of North Carolina. The old brick structure on Catholic Hill became the first public school for blacks in Western North Carolina.

In Asheville it generally has been true that private school education has been better than public, that education for women has surpassed that for men, and that the Methodists, Presbyterians, Episcopalians, and Catholics provided the best instruction of all, if only for a privileged few.

The first public school opened in Asheville on January 16, 1888, enrolling 450 white and over 380 black students. Since only grades one through five were included, "pupils of higher grades were turned away, many weeping in the bitterness of their disappointment." For the first two years, schools were kept open only ninety-two days, primarily because of a lack of funds and an outbreak of scarlet fever in 1890. That same year Asheville's public schools enrolled more than 1,100 students,

Above: *"Cyclone Mack" McClendon, a revival preacher in Asheville between 1910 and 1927, conducted services in a tent on West Haywood Street at Cumberland Avenue. Known for his booming voice, McClendon frequently broadcast radio programs, including famous fights, to listening crowds on Main Street. Courtesy, Ewart Ball Collection, Southern Highlands, UNC-Asheville*

Facing page, top, right: *There was great diversity in religion in Asheville and the surrounding area. Ashevillians were mainly of Protestant and Catholic faith. Outside the city one found the fundamental religions of the mountaineers. Baptisms by the Holiness people, such as this one in 1909, typically took place in the rivers and creeks surrounding the city. (NCDAH)*

Facing page, top, far right: *Francis Asbury became bishop of the Methodist Church in 1784. His travels from Maine to South Carolina carried him along the Drover's Road in Western North Carolina. The journal Asbury kept of his visits to Asheville proved to be valuable as a local history of the area. (NCDAH)*

Facing page, bottom: *Students in the industrial arts program of the Asheville Normal and Collegiate Institute build a lean-to addition in 1915. Courtesy, North Carolina Collection, Pack Memorial Library*

580 white and 520 black.

Until 1908 white teachers' salaries in Asheville averaged thirty dollars a month. Black instructors were paid eighteen dollars a month. Teachers purchased their own classroom supplies, usually a blackboard, crayon, chalk, writing instruments, and report cards, if any were given out. Teachers were also expected to give out a treat, usually a piece of candy, at the end of a school day.

Ashevillians' conduct toward public education indicated a divided opinion. The first tax levy to operate a public school system in Asheville passed eight years after the North Carolina legislature authorized it in 1879. The parents of students who attended private schools and many of those who were against the idea of a general education "for all races and stations in life" fought against the school tax. Still, supporters of the tax levy won by a clear majority. So completely had opinion changed by 1906 that voters overwhelmingly approved a law making it compulsory for city children between the ages of eight and fourteen to attend school. Also included were those who were between fourteen and sixteen and who were not regularly employed. The Asheville city school system became one of the first in the nation to adopt a compulsory attendance law.

Asheville's school system enjoyed its greatest boom from 1901 to 1929. The school board quickly purchased the old Asheville Military Academy on Academy Street. A public school for blacks opened on Beaumont Street. Between 1919 and 1926 Ashevillians approved more than two million dollars in bonds for new schools. For whites, Claxton, Vance, Hall Fletcher, and Eugene Rankin were built. Livingston Street, Burton Street, Mountain Street, and Stephens-Lee were constructed for blacks. A new building went up on the site of the old Newton Academy on Biltmore Avenue. To cap the system, a high school was constructed on McDowell Street in 1929 at a cost of more than one million dollars. There would be no more significant construction of schools in Asheville for more than thirty years.

Started as an adult vocational education center in Asheville in 1959, Asheville-Buncombe Technical College has grown into a multipurpose institution that now serves a student body of over 3,400 students. A-B Tech's growth has been spectacular. Since its inception in 1968, the registered nurse program at A-B Tech proportionately has passed more students on the national licensing examination than any two- or four-year institution in the state. More than 90 percent of Tech's nursing graduates pass the stringent exam. Under its two presidents, Thomas Simpson and Harley Haynes, the institution established exceptional programs in engineering technology and a wide variety of fields in vocational education. In terms of Western North Carolina's industrial development, A-B Tech has led the way with mechanical and civil engineering programs. A-B Tech boasts some of the region's most sophisticated tech-

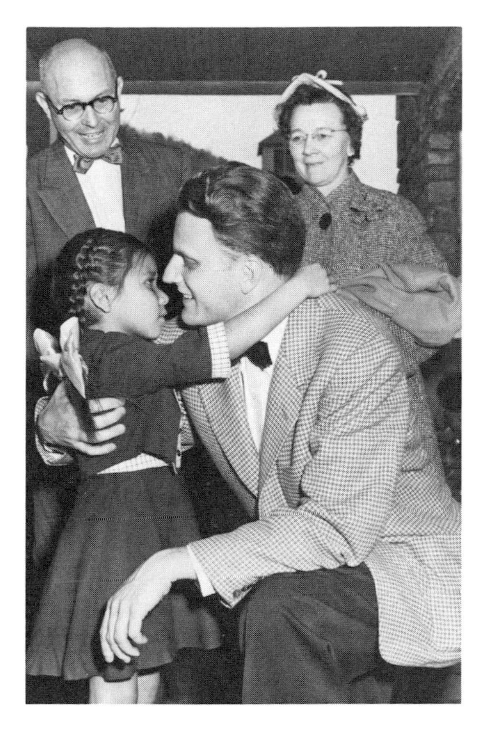

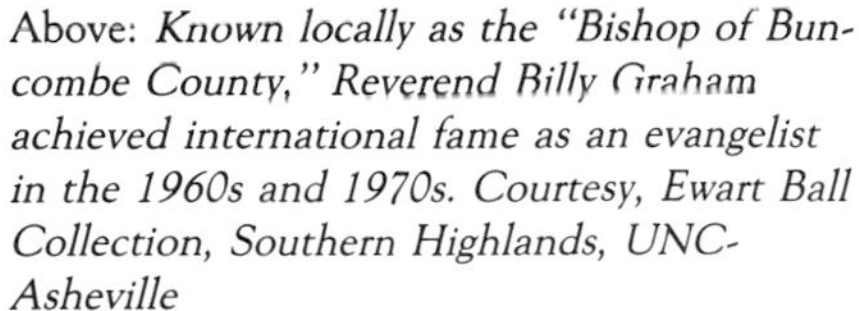

Above: *Known locally as the "Bishop of Buncombe County," Reverend Billy Graham achieved international fame as an evangelist in the 1960s and 1970s. Courtesy, Ewart Ball Collection, Southern Highlands, UNC-Asheville*

Above, right: *Members of the Asheville Shakespeare Club pose together circa 1903. Top row, left to right: Bessie Lee, Daisy McDowell Ligon, Lillian Reynolds, and Mrs. Courtney. Middle row, left to right: Min Rorison, Nancy Grant, Mabel Smith Walker, Mally Erwin, Sarah Rorison Rawls, Blanche Wood, and Aileen Reynolds Ball. Bottom row, left to right: Nellie F. Morrison, Lottie Cobb, and Nan Erwin. Courtesy, North Carolina Collection, Pack Memorial Library*

Facing page, top: *William Sidney Porter, better known as O. Henry, married Sara Lindsey Coleman from Weaverville and lived and wrote in Asheville in 1909. He is buried in Riverside Cemetery in Asheville. Courtesy, Ewart Ball Collection, Southern Highlands, UNC-Asheville*

Facing page, bottom: *Asheville lawyer, historian, and bibliophile Forster A. Sondley bequeathed his personal library of 40,000 volumes to the city. Courtesy, North Carolina Collection, Pack Memorial Library*

nology in computer-aided design and manufacturing and in robotics.

The University of North Carolina at Asheville began as Buncombe County Junior College in 1927. In 1963 the college became a four-year institution and in 1969 Asheville-Biltmore was reorganized as the University of North Carolina at Asheville, a part of the university system of North Carolina.

From a small student body of 800 in 1969 the university has grown to more than 3,500 students today. Since 1980 it has been the fastest growing campus of the university system, and one of the most rapidly expanding institutions in the United States. Part of the university's success lies in the fact that it combines a rigorous liberal arts requirement with novel and traditional programs. Under two presidents, William Highsmith and David Brown, the university quickly has become a first-rate institution of higher learning. In the midst of a capital expansion that will double its size by 1990, the university will mature into a regional learning center.

Almost two centuries after he first visited Asheville, the Reverend George Newton would likely approve of the city's mind and spirit today. Surrounded by religious retreats of almost every major denomination and possessing two of the state's better institutions of higher education, Asheville seems well on its way to fulfilling Newton's dream of a well-educated and pious public.

CHAPTER IX

Thomas Wolfe's Asheville

Facing page: *In 1909 the courthouse, fire department, police station, and city market were located in the massive building standing on the east end of Pack Square. This was the square Thomas Wolfe knew as a young boy and wrote about in his first novel* Look Homeward, Angel. *The townspeople Wolfe watched from the window of his father's monument shop, located to the right of the courthouse, served as the characters in this locally controversial book. Courtesy, Thomas Wolfe Collection, Pack Memorial Library*

Between 1890 and 1910 Thomas Wolfe's Asheville of *Look Homeward, Angel* was born. It was a city of eight magnificent hotels, twenty-two health resorts, and more than fifty boardinghouses. The North Carolina general assembly officially designated Asheville a city in 1883. The population stood at 3,874, but with thousands of tourists, promoters, and homesteaders streaming into the region on the newly completed rail line, it would soon grow to 50,193 by 1927. There it would remain for fifty years. From his vantage point on Court Square, a young Tom Wolfe watched the city grow to maturity by 1916.

A new courthouse dominated the city's center in 1877. Symbolic of Asheville's new dignity, it contained an opera house seating 400 on the third floor. A new street railway brought passengers from the railway depot on the French Broad River to Court Square where carriages whisked them away to hotels, hospitals, and homes. The square became the transportation center of the city.

Asheville had its first telephone exchange in 1883 and a brand new national bank the same year. Ten physicians, one woman among them, six dentists, five real estate agencies, and more than twenty-one lawyers' firms practiced in the city and county. Fifteen contracting companies and fifty general merchandise houses built and supplied the needs of a developing regional economy. Brick structures replaced wooden ones around the square and along Main Street and Patton Avenue. Two to four stories high, stores and businesses featured imposing fronts of glass and iron.

Liquor dealers, quacks, and druggists abounded, especially around the main square, and patent-medicine men such as W.C. Carmichael and Westray Battle made small fortunes peddling their creations to tourists and patients at the sanitoriums around the city. Downtown was still lit by kerosene lamps, and the sewage system consisted of "old man McNabb" who made the rounds in a horse-drawn wagon with a huge wooden barrel in back.

In 1890 at the intersection of Coxe and Patton avenues was one of the finest gambling establishments and brothels of the era. Mountaineers loved to gamble. A circus that came to town in 1901 with its con men and "card sharpies" swindled locals at the Eagle Hotel annex out of more than $32,000 and "eight good horses." Hotly pursued by an angry mob of townspeople, the circus left several animals behind on Court Square, including a caged leopard, as they hastily made their way south to Spartanburg.

There were no street signs or caution lights in Asheville in the 1880s. None were necessary. However, the new city decided to give streets names and do away with the confusion of local designations. Streets were named for well-known figures in Western North Carolina history, for trees and their foliage, and for geographical and topical features. Closer to town, many modest streets suddenly became pretentious avenues.

Before 1910 west Asheville consisted chiefly of pastures and farmland. The coming of street railways created a separate township annexed by Asheville in 1917 in a closely contested election. Furious at charges they had manipulated the election, city officials retaliated by giving innocuous state names to west Asheville's streets and roads, thus robbing them of their former distinctiveness.

Farther east, James M. "Jake" Chiles developed Kenilworth Forest. Enchanted by the world of Sir Walter Scott and inspired by the extraordinarily beautiful stands of birch, hickory, oak, and chestnut trees on the hills overlooking Biltmore Avenue, Chiles recreated a mythical Scotland in Asheville by giving Kenilworth's streets names such as Essex, Dorchester, and Leicester. Built partially of granite boulders from the mountains, Kenilworth Inn became a favorite winter resort of the wealthy.

In February 1889 Asheville decided to improve its streets to make way for a new railway system. Electricity was chosen over steam because the city fathers feared pollution. Court Square was paved and six miles of streets macadamized. Older streets were widened. Asheville voted $625,000 in street improvements in 1892, an enormous expenditure for its day. The streetcar line was extended southwest to Sulphur Springs, the rail line to Murphy was finished, a new city hall and market was built on east Court Square, and a new post office was erected at the corner of Patton Avenue and Haywood Street.

Probably the most important event in the development of Asheville as a city was the formation of the Board of Trade in 1889. The board's mission was to promote Asheville's image as a modern, progressive city. Its motto was "Transportation and Trade." Composed of sixty-five of Asheville and Buncombe County's best-known civic and business leaders, the board pushed for the development of agriculture, good roads throughout the region, and better schools, parks, and recreation facilities for the city and county.

Finished in 1905, Riverside Park became the city's most celebrated park. Located in the flat plain across from Riverside Cemetery, the park's facilities were the most magnificent the city has ever had. They consisted of a large exposition pavilion, a boathouse, daily canoe and sailboat excursions on the French Broad, a penny arcade, a merry-go-round, stables at the far end with weekly horse shows, and an elaborate baseball field where the Skylanders (later the Mountaineers and finally

Facing page, top, right: *Before the Civil War, moonshining was not illegal in Western North Carolina. When a revenue was later placed on the homemade liquor, mountaineers like this 1910 man hid their stills, and Pack Square became the center for illegal moonshine traffic. (NCDAH)*

Facing page, top, far right: *Destroyed by fire in April 1909, the original Kenilworth Inn was built in the Gothic style in 1890 by Jake Chiles. The second inn (pictured here), rebuilt on the same site, was a neo-Tudor building. During World Wars I and II, the Kenilworth Inn served as a United States Naval Hospital and today is a mental hospital known as Appalachian Hall. Courtesy, Ewart Ball Collection, Southern Highlands, UNC-Asheville*

Facing page, bottom: *Asheville's first telephone exchange was established in 1883. By 1920, when this photo was taken, the exchange employed more than 250 women in the Asheville location. Courtesy, Ewart Ball Collection, Southern Highlands, UNC-Asheville*

the Tourists) played only daylight games. Thomas Wolfe recalled the excitement of Sunday afternoons watching ladies dressed in silks and satins with plumes in their hats, riding sidesaddle on the park's outer ring.

Riverside featured an artificial lake with a small island in the center. Motion pictures were shown twice weekly on a giant screen erected on the island while moonlight boaters drifted between island and shore watching the performances of early silent screen stars such as Flora Finch and John Bunny.

South of the city, Oates Park on Southside Avenue housed Asheville's professional baseball team after the 1911 flood damaged Riverside's field. Oates was one of the finest baseball facilities in the South. Touring teams such as the Philadelphia Athletics and the Boston Red Sox arrived by streetcar for exhibition games between 1912 and 1922. In 1915 the Mountaineers won the championship of the North Carolina (Class D) league and afterward came in second for three straight years. Eventually the team moved to McCormick field, one of the first parks with lights, and Oates became the home of Asheville's black professional baseball team.

Instrumental in bringing a new post office to Asheville in 1931, Jeter C. Pritchard was honored by the people of Asheville when the site of the old post office was named Pritchard Park. Elected to the United States Senate in 1895, Pritchard filled the vacancy caused by the death of Zebulon Baird Vance. Senator Pritchard authored the first legislation introduced in the United States to establish a National Forest Reservation in the Appalachias. Courtesy, North Carolina Collection, Pack Memorial Library

In 1890 Bingham Military Academy moved to Asheville from Mebane in the central part of the state. Located north of the city across from Riverside Park, Bingham Academy added ceremony and pageantry to turn-of-the-century Asheville. Every Saturday afternoon the cadet corps filed through Montford on their way to Pack Square. The marching cadets often mustered in the evening at the old Battery Park Hotel ballroom for a dinner dance. One observer noted that the "cadets and young women of Asheville were especially regular in attendance. They loved the Blue Danube Waltz."

Three men—one a philanthropist, another a politician, and the last a businessman—transformed Victorian Asheville into the modern progressive city of the roaring twenties. As a modern city, Asheville originated in their actions and ideas.

A wealthy lumberman from Cleveland, George Willis Pack was at first horrified by the city's "filth and ignorance." When he moved to Asheville in 1880, Pack leased rooms at the newly built Swannanoa Hotel. Offended at the lack of "sanitary facilities" at the hotel, Pack insisted that the manager install a bathroom. A tub was imported, a reservoir rigged to furnish water, and an entire room remodeled for Pack's convenience. When the room was completed, he held a "public toilet" and invited Asheville's business and social leaders to see the newest idea in "progressive living and comfort."

Pack next proposed that Court Square be cleaned up. In the 1880s the area was a squalid square of mud and refuse. Several days each week farmers spilled over onto the square, parking their wagons and ox carts and selling their goods from buckboards. Court Square attracted scores

Built in 1912, the Majestic Theater featured such films as The Love Light, *with Mary Pickford. Admission to the theater was thirty cents for adults and ten cents for children. Courtesy, Ewart Ball Collection, Southern Highlands, UNC-Asheville*

of people who lived downtown over stores in rooms and apartments. Lawyers and spectators gathered around the courthouse on court days. To add to the confusion, streetcars daily disgorged hundreds of visitors and tourists onto the square.

Along with Charles D. Blanton and Virgil Lusk, Pack persuaded the city fathers in 1890 to move the courthouse over to College Street, light the square with electric bulbs, pave it with bricks, and open it up for pedestrians by placing sidewalks, benches, and a fountain in the middle. To inspire civic pride and virtue in mountaineers, he contributed more than one half of the $3,000 necessary to erect a monument on the square to Zebulon Vance.

Pack also purchased the First National Bank building on the square and presented it to the Library Association for use as a "public library and reading room." He gave a tract of almost two acres facing College Street on the south side of the square to Buncombe County to be used as a site for a new courthouse erected in 1902. Determined to keep farmers and their livestock from the square, Pack prevailed upon the city to authorize a market in the basement of city hall in 1892 and to prohibit unlicensed vendors from the square altogether. Disgruntled farmers moved their wagons to Lexington Street, and, under the leadership of James McClure, organized still another curb market that eventually survived the city's. A small farmers' market remained at the foot of

Above: *One of Asheville's greatest benefactors, George Willis Pack donated land for the site of a new county courthouse and for several parks built around the city. He also purchased the First National Bank building and gave it to the city to use as a library. Pack Memorial Library stood on the square which also bears his name. Courtesy, North Carolina Collection, Pack Memorial Library*

Right: *The board of directors of the North Carolina Federation of Women's Clubs pose at the home of Mrs. W.F. Cocke on South French Broad Avenue in 1911. By 1905, Asheville had become a favorite meeting place of clubs and organizations throughout the state. Courtesy, North Carolina Collection, Pack Memorial Library*

Facing page, top: *The Asheville Tourists baseball team played in the Class B South Atlantic League from 1924 until 1930. McCormick Field was the home of the Tourists and was not lighted until the 1930 season. Courtesy, North Carolina Collection, Pack Memorial Library*

Facing page, bottom: *The football team of the Bingham School is ready for action circa 1900. Colonel Robert Bingham moved the school from Mebane to Asheville in 1891. The school closed in 1928. Courtesy, North Carolina Collection, Pack Memorial Library*

Lexington Street until the state erected a new one south of the city in 1980.

Heedful of the gangs of children who swarmed over the square, Pack bought a plat of land on the west side of South French Broad Avenue, donating it to the city to be maintained as a children's playground. Today it is called Aston Park. Pack started the city's first kindergarten, paying the salaries of two black teachers for the school on Beaumont Street and half the salaries of other teachers throughout the city. Because of his urging, a public school system was adopted in 1889. In a very real sense, George W. Pack was the father of the city's first public school system. A grateful city renamed the square in his honor.

As mayor from 1889 to 1893, politician Charles Blanton, inspired by Pack's progressive ideas, determined to reform Asheville and make it the finest city in the state. Efficiency and morality became Blanton's criteria for reform. Under Blanton gambling and prostitution, always operating openly within the city, were outlawed.

Twelve brothels and "gaming establishments" were closed. Offended by "that damned reformer," prostitutes and gamblers simply removed the familiar red lights from the front windows along Patton, Lexington, and Biltmore, and installed them in rear windows. Saloons, always numerous in Asheville, were licensed and heavily taxed. Few closed.

Blanton also hoped to improve city services. At his urging, a city

26
27
605

GOODES DRUG STORE
SODA

Above: *Richmond Pearson, a North Carolina and United States representative who made his home in Asheville, served as an American minister to Greece, Persia, and Montenegro under the administration of Theodore Roosevelt. Courtesy, North Carolina Collection, Pack Memorial Library*

Facing page, top: *By 1890 there were twenty tobacco dealers and six warehouses in Asheville. It was predicted the city would become the tobacco center of North Carolina. Courtesy, Ewart Ball Collection, Southern Highlands, UNC-Asheville*

Facing page, bottom: *Led by a Confederate veteran, the Thirtieth Division parades down Patton Avenue in 1920. The portable archway in the background was constructed in 1918 and used for many parade reunions. Courtesy, Ewart Ball Collection, Southern Highlands, UNC-Asheville*

board of health was created to supervise and enforce sanitation in food and water supplies, cafes and restaurants, and hotels and boardinghouses. Much to the despair of Asheville's famed patent medicine men, drugs, medicines, and druggists were included in the ordinance. During Blanton's administration Pack Square and the streets around it were paved and sidewalks of stones, bricks, and boards were raised on downtown avenues. A strong advocate of public transportation, Blanton also helped bring the first streetcar railway to Asheville.

To Blanton, a modern, progressive city needed an efficient, effective government to deliver services to its citizens. To him and to many Ashevillians of the 1890s, the old division of the city into four political wards presided over by bosses promoted corruption and cronyism and needed to be replaced. After one of the most turbulent, inflamed campaigns in the city's history, Blanton finally compromised. For the next forty years, Asheville was governed by a six-member city council, four from the older wards and two elected at large, plus a mayor elected separately. In a gentleman's agreement, Blanton and his progressive supporters conceded that one of the new council members should be black, the other Jewish.

For his part, businessman Dr. Edwin Grove intended to change Asheville from a seasonal tourist town to a regional shopping and convention center. His purchase of the old Battery Park Hotel in 1921 was the key to his plan to transform the city's downtown area. Grove wanted to tear down the old Victorian hotel, construct a modern one in its place, erect a magnificent indoor arcade across from the new Battery Park complex, and enclose the whole as a downtown plaza. The park and wandering paths surrounding the old hotel would be replaced by shops and a new civic center. The new Battery Park Hotel and the arcade across from it were but the first steps in Grove's grand scheme for downtown Asheville.

All the reforms and projects of progressive Asheville were threatened by the great flood of 1916, perhaps the city's greatest natural disaster. The rains began on July 8 and continued without let up for a week. At 4:10 on Sunday morning, July 16, the Swannanoa River leaped its banks and spread outward as it headed toward Biltmore Village and the French Broad. Later that same morning, earthen dams broke at Kanuga and Osceola lakes in Henderson County, sending a ten-foot wall of water down Mud Creek into the French Broad River toward Asheville. By 6:00 a.m. the two rivers came together to send a tidal wave into the city's waterfront, smashing lumberyards, tobacco warehouses, freight yards, oil storage tanks, railroad tracks, hotels, and businesses as it lurched northward. At first light the French Broad flowed more than fifteen feet deep through Biltmore and was more than a mile wide. North of Asheville, most of Weaver Dam was swept away and generators in the power plant supplying electricity to the city short-circuited. Almost

all electricity to the city was gone by mid-day. Full power would not be restored until the first of August. By the afternoon of July 16, Asheville effectively was cut off from the rest of the world. All bridges over the two rivers from Black Mountain to Marshall were gone, telegraph lines were down, and rail lines were washed out. For the next two weeks, the city experienced severe food and oil shortages. It would not be until August 4 that the first train returned from Spartanburg.

In all, twenty-nine died during the flood, eleven in Asheville. The riverfront never fully recovered. Some warehouses and businesses were not rebuilt, the new depot didn't seem as grand as the old one, the Glen Rock never again was the same, and, perhaps the greatest casualty of all, Riverside Park was gone forever.

Still, the 1916 flood only dampened the spirits of Ashevillians. In the midst of a banking and real estate boom that seemed to go on forever, the city turned its attention to the flood of visitors who returned in the

Above, left: *Purchased in 1921 by E.W. Grove, the old Battery Park Hotel was demolished and the mountain on which it sat was leveled. The new Battery Park Hotel (pictured), a highrise brick structure, opened its doors to tourists in 1924. Today the Battery Park serves as an apartment building for senior citizens. Courtesy, Ewart Ball Collection, Southern Highlands, UNC-Asheville*

Top: *On Sunday, July 16, 1916, the water level of the French Broad River rose to twenty feet. Hardest hit was Biltmore Village where the river was almost a mile wide. (NCDAH)*

Above: *The Southern Railway Station (left), streetcars, and many Asheville businesses suffered great losses during the 1916 flood. Courtesy, North Carolina Collection, Pack Memorial Library*

Top: *Eight years after the publication of his first novel,* Look Homeward, Angel, *Thomas Wolfe returned to his hometown. The similarities between the fictional characters in his book and the people of Asheville created such a controversy he feared for his life. For a few months in 1937 Wolfe stayed in a cabin just outside of Asheville. There he wrote of his homecoming and why* You Can't Go Home Again. *Courtesy, Thomas Wolfe Collection, Pack Memorial Library*

Above: *Operating for sixty-five years from the same office on Rankin Avenue, the Western Union boys on bicycles were described by Thomas Wolfe in his first novel* Look Homeward, Angel. *Courtesy, Ewart Ball Collection, Southern Highlands, UNC-Asheville*

fall of 1916. Fed by a bust in the Florida land boom and an expanding regional economy, boosters, bankers, and boomers, or, as Tom Wolfe refered to them, "the binder boys," rushed into the mountains. As Wolfe remembered it, everyone prospered. "It was fantastic!" he recalled, "Everyone was a real estate man . . . barbers, lawyers, clothiers . . . . And there seemed to be only one rule . . . buy, always to buy . . . and to sell again within any two days at any price . . . . When the supply of streets and houses was exhausted, new streets were . . . created in the surrounding wilderness; and even before these streets were paved or a house had been built upon them, the land was being sold, and then resold, by the acre, by the foot, for hundreds of thousands of dollars."

After forty booming years, Asheville's prosperity seemed permanent.

UNCLE SAM'S
LOAN OFFICE
CLOTHING
DIAMONDS
WATCHES
DAILY 10:30 2:30 7:30
AUCTION SALE
DAILY 10:30 2:30 7:30
OF UNREDEEMED PLEDGES
JAY MEARS
UP STAIRS
SHOE STORE
EVERY
UNREDEEMED PLEDGE IN THE HOUSE
PUBLIC AUCTION
10:30
HARRY ROSE
LICENSED TO SELL JEWELRY
PUBLIC AUCTION
CONDUCTING
OLYMPIA
CANDY
KITCHEN

CHAPTER X

The Long Depression

Facing page, top: *Uncle Sam's Loan Office located on Pack Square held frequent auctions, most of them as well attended as this 1929 event. Courtesy, Ewart Ball Collection, Southern Highlands, UNC-Asheville*

Asheville went bust on November 9, 1930. At 9:00 on "Black Thursday" morning, the city's four major banks closed their doors to the public, thus beginning a Depression that, to many mountaineers, seemed without end.

The collapse of the real estate market three years earlier foretold the coming disaster. After 1920 Asheville fell heir to an unprecedented speculation in real estate which paralleled the great Florida "flat land" boom and came during a period of national prosperity. Spurred on by Floridians, real estate agents created even larger developments throughout Western North Carolina. Standing on Laurel Mountain twenty miles south of Asheville, the Fleetwood Hotel rose to become more than twelve stories of fabled air castle. Its skeleton soon would haunt speculators and bankers for years to come. To the east, Hollywood, an enormous subdivision planned for Black Mountain, collapsed, leaving only an elaborately carved entrance gate and a few half-paved streets in its wake. In Asheville, Kenilworth's lake and grounds were never finished. The Grove Arcade suffered a similar fate. Conceived in 1921 when downtown Asheville was expanding, the Arcade stood almost empty. By 1930 over 230 stores and 1,800 homes in Asheville were vacant. Less than 15 percent of the office space in the city was occupied.

Ashevillians seemed ill-prepared to cope with the Depression. Between 1920 and 1928 the city's population had grown by 79 percent to just over 50,000. Only Charlotte and Winston-Salem had experienced greater increases. Having already eclipsed Raleigh and Wilmington, Asheville seemed destined to surpass Durham and Greensboro to become the state's third largest city.

Asheville borrowed heavily in the 1920s to expand and pay for city services. By 1929 municipal bonds totaling more than $16,000,000 had been issued. While Charlotte, Raleigh, Durham, Greensboro, High Point, and Wilmington borrowed money for similar purposes, Asheville's indebtedness differed from other North Carolina cities.

First, Asheville catered to the visitor seeking recreation and health. Thus, the city spent large sums on public parks, on landscaping Battery Park hill and the new city-county plaza, and on planting trees and shrubs. A new municipal golf course was built and new streets opened and paved. Begun in 1928, the spectacular Rhododendron Festival was yet another of Asheville's lures. The results of a city made more attractive to outsiders seemed at that time to justify the expense.

Above: *The east end of Pack Square went through many changes in the 1920s and 1930s. (NCDAH)*

Facing page, top: *Asheville's first skyscraper, the Jackson Building, was built on the site of W.O. Wolfe's monument shop. Wolfe's wife, Julia, purchased the land in 1883 for $1,000 and sold it in 1922 for $30,000. The fifteen-story Jackson Building, designed by architect Ronald Greene, was built in the pointed Gothic style. Courtesy, Ewart Ball Collection, Southern Highlands, UNC-Asheville*

Facing page, bottom, right: *City hall (right) was built between 1926 and 1928. Architect Douglas D. Ellington originally planned a twin building for the county with a connecting one-story bus terminal but county officials didn't like Ellington's unique idea. The classical style, seventeen-story structure (left) was chosen for the courthouse. Courtesy, Ewart Ball Collection, Southern Highlands, UNC-Asheville*

Facing page, bottom, far right: *Spiral staircases in the Grove Arcade Building connect the first floor to the second floor's open balconies. Constructed in 1926 to serve as a shopping mall and office building for the downtown area, the arcade now houses the National Climatic Data Center. Courtesy, Ewart Ball Collection, Southern Highlands, UNC-Asheville*

Two projects reflected Asheville's aspirations just before the great crash. Finished in 1928 by Douglas Ellington, a colossal city hall dominated the city's skyline. The new city building together with the adjacent county courthouse stood out as monuments to Asheville's boundless optimism of the 1920s. Planned by Ellington to complement each other, the two buildings would give Asheville and Buncombe County the finest municipal facilities in the south. In 1926, many Ashevillians thought that within a decade the city would rival Richmond or Atlanta.

The collection of taxes began to fall rapidly after 1922 even as expenses mounted. Faced with raising funds to construct new public works and the necessity of paying debts on assessment bonds, Asheville began to issue and sell municipal bonds.

Before 1922 all the bonds issued by the city totaled only $2,861,300. By early 1930 the level of indebtedness reached $18,786,500. When the Central Bank and Trust closed its doors on November 9, the sum had reached $23,600,000. Of the eight largest cities in the state, Asheville's indebtedness was the highest. In fact, Asheville's debt was larger than that of Raliegh, Durham, Greensboro, and Winston-Salem combined.

Faced with declining revenues and mounting indebtedness, Asheville refused to curtail city services, call off its ambitious building program, or reduce overall expenses in a significant way. To city officials, the debt problem seemed temporary. Certainly, continued growth, expansion, and annexation would create additional sources of revenue and alleviate the problem. After all, there had not been an economic recession since 1893.

Asheville's situation became critical after 1927. When the real estate boom collapsed in 1926, the Central Bank and Trust Company, Western North Carolina's largest bank with more than $18 million in deposits, found itself holding millions of dollars in real estate loans secured by badly depreciated paper. Afraid that foreclosure on the loans would bankrupt many local businesses and wreck Asheville's economy, the bank's officers persuaded city and county officials to leave more than six million dollars in cash deposits at Central while they operated on the proceeds of short-term notes. It was a decision that ruined Asheville for years to come.

Although North Carolina required municipal deposits to be secured by adequate collateral, Central Bank instead put up depreciated real estate notes at inflated pre-1927 prices. In 1928, state bank examiners declared Central effectively insolvent, but the state banking commission did little except notify city officials. The report was kept secret, and the bank continued its operations. Between 1928 and 1930 Central stayed open only through deposits from Asheville and Buncombe County and by falsifying its books. The end came in November 1930.

Central Bank and Trust's closing sent shock waves throughout Buncombe County, Western North Carolina, and, indeed, all of North Car-

Facing page, top, right: *The George Vanderbilt Hotel was built in 1924 by a group of Asheville businessmen. The hotel still stands today on Haywood Street beside the Asheville Civic Center and is known as the Vanderbilt Apartments. Like the Battery Park Hotel, the Vanderbilt serves as a senior citizen apartment building. Courtesy, Ewart Ball Collection, Southern Highlands, UNC-Asheville*

Facing page, top, far right: *The engraving department of the* Asheville Citizen-Times *used this equipment circa 1930s. Courtesy, Ewart Ball Collection, Southern Highlands, UNC-Asheville*

Facing page, bottom: *Pack Square buzzed with activity during the boom period of the 1920s. It was dominated by the Vance Monument (right), completed in 1898 in memory of Governor Zebulon Baird Vance. Courtesy, Ewart Ball Collection, Southern Highlands, UNC-Asheville*

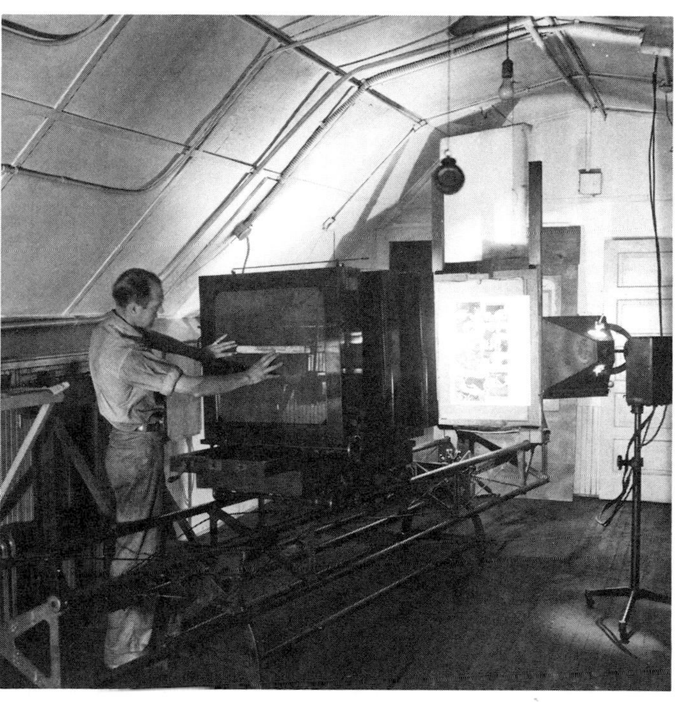

RAYS STUDIO
VANCE

HOOD
TIRES
HOOD
HAYES & HOPSON.
HYVIS
HOOD
TIRES
FIX PUNCTURES
FIX PUNCTURES
HAYES

LIC SCHOOLS
NOT FOR SELF BUT FOR OTHERS
ASHEVILLE
KLAN No. 4

Facing page, top: *A large crowd gathered on Pack Square to watch the fire at the Emporium department store on July 25, 1923. The Emporium was located beside the old Pack Memorial Library. Courtesy, Ewart Ball Collection, Southern Highlands, UNC-Asheville*

Facing page, bottom, far left: *Located on the south end of Coxe Avenue, Hayes and Hopson is one of Asheville's oldest continuing service stations. Courtesy, Ewart Ball Collection, Southern Highlands, UNC-Asheville*

Facing page, bottom, left: *The Asheville Ku Klux Klan advocated free public schools in 1925. Between 1920 and 1925, the KKK dominated Buncombe County politics, endorsing progressive civic issues as well as reactionary social positions. Courtesy, North Carolina Collection, Pack Memorial Library*

olina. Within two days eleven cooperating banks in six surrounding counties also closed their doors. City and county governments lost more than $6.5 million in deposits. Deprived of operating funds and unable to sell more bonds, Asheville defaulted on all its debt payments, closing the market to city bonds and securities on May 1, 1931.

An angry public soon forced all the city's officials to resign and demanded an immediate curtailment of spending. While a Buncombe County grand jury began hearing evidence and returning indictments against those involved in the Central Bank swindle, Asheville's ordeal intensified. Two of those indicted, the former mayor and a Central Bank officer, committed suicide, while still another bank official failed in his attempt and was committed instead to a state mental hospital. Tried and convicted on a number of charges ranging from violations of state banking regulations to embezzlement, the Central Bank's president was sent to prison. Furious at the revelation that the state banking commission knew that Central was insolvent as early as 1928, the Buncombe grand jury quickly returned charges against three North Carolina commission members for malfeasance in office.

Asheville's default exposed the city's unsound financial structure and its extensive involvement in local banking institutions. An outraged public immediately demanded a new leadership and a refinancing of the debt to restore public confidence. To many Ashevillians, the debt problem still seemed temporary, the Depression only a setback of short duration. Many thought that by simply tinkering with the machinery of government, by throwing the shysters out of city hall, and by restoring public confidence, the crisis would soon be past. Few realized that, for Asheville, the problems caused by the Depression would last for fifty years.

In May 1931, six months after the banks closed, a discredited city government was replaced by a new manager-council administration. Under the new authority, city government was reorganized under a city manager who supervised budget expenditures. No longer were departments autonomously controlled and funded. Operating expenses were drastically reduced. Efficiency and resourcefulness became the standards for city government after 1931.

On August 12, 1931, Asheville's total indebtedness reached $23,000,000. With its proportionate share of the county debt included, the city now owed more than $41,000,000. Asheville plainly could not meet principal and interest payments on such a vast sum. Thus, over the next four months, city officials met with representatives of bond and note holders in an effort to renegotiate the debt.

It was agreed that there would be no reduction in the principal of the debt. Two series of bonds would be exchanged for all outstanding notes and bonds. To discharge the debt, percentage limitations were placed on allowances for city services and a specified sum was set aside to pay for the new bonds.

In order to limit future indebtedness, city council specified that as long as any of the refunding bonds remained outstanding, no new liabilities, other than that represented by tax anticipation notes, could be incurred in excess of 20 percent of the city's assessed valuation, unless the new debts were approved by a majority of the voters in an authorized referendum. This way, Asheville would not be able to repeat the mistakes of the 1920s nor could the new administration issue bonds without public knowledge and approval. Thus restrained, Asheville faced forty years of trial and hardship. The last portion of the city's refunded Depression debt was paid on October 28, 1976.

Planned as a city of parks, plazas, squares, and hotels Asheville gradually broke down as the Depression worsened. Some Ashevillians vaguely blamed "conditions." Others developed a deep distrust of government and business, especially banks. On weekdays farmers peddled apples, corn, and firewood on every road leading to the city. Hungry men stood in long lines in front of the soup kitchen on Pack Square. Scores of hoboes and jobless men swarmed around the depot near the river and gradually drifted toward downtown.

Still, some enterprises flourished. More Ashevillians than ever went to the movie theaters on Pack Square and Biltmore Avenue. Smoking and chewing tobacco increased, perhaps as a relief for hunger. Drugstores on Pack Square reported growing sales of contraceptives and candy. Pack Library noted a significant increase in circulation, and Atwater Kent radios sold well.

Residents of Asheville and Buncombe County fared better than most North Carolinians during the Depression. Massive public works projects, especially on the Blue Ridge Parkway, and the opening of a new rayon plant in Enka helped to keep unemployment relatively low in Asheville and Buncombe County.

Asheville and Buncombe County undertook relief projects late in 1931. Asheville paid married men $1.50 to $2.50 a day to cut firewood, plant trees, maintain streets, and clean up the city. A wood yard for the needy was opened on Broadway. Most of the work on Pritchard Park was done by work-relief laborers, and, in black neighborhoods, community gardens for the poor were started. Despite this, relief efforts were inadequate until the federal government intervened and provided assistance with the Federal Relief Act of 1932. By 1933 unemployed families in Asheville still received an average of only sixteen dollars per month, barely enough for subsistence.

Yet optimism briefly flourished in the midst of the Depression. The *Asheville Times* sponsored a community campaign centered around the theme of why Western North Carolinians should "have faith in Asheville." In his winning essay, Herbert Miles urged Ashevillians to "have faith in yourself . . . in Asheville . . . and . . . have patience! We are not being singled out for trouble or punishment . . . . Let us pay the Piper

Facing page, right: *During his visit to Asheville in 1936, President Franklin D. Roosevelt stayed at the Grove Park Inn. While touring Western North Carolina, Roosevelt stopped off at the Quallah Reservation to meet some Cherokee Indians. Courtesy, Ewart Ball Collection, Southern Highlands, UNC-Asheville*

Facing page, far right: *Nearing completion of construction in 1928, Beaucatcher Tunnel would connect east and west Asheville. It took four years to build the tunnel which rerouted traffic from the old route down the Swannanoa River to Biltmore. Courtesy, Ewart Ball Collection, Southern Highlands, UNC-Asheville*

for we have danced! And we shall dance again." It was time, Miles maintained, to forget "the bad old days" and set about rebuilding the city's fortunes.

Certainly, Asheville tried. A new post office was opened in 1930 and Pritchard Park dug out and landscaped in 1931. A new city auditorium was planned. The tunnel through Beaucatcher Mountain opened in 1930 and the city council proudly proclaimed it Asheville's "new main street." Even in the grim months of 1932, Asheville never relaxed in its efforts to lure summer people to the city. Almost every civic and merchants' organization steadfastly supported and promoted the idea of a Blue Ridge parkway in 1934 and of a new national park to the west in 1933. Begun before the Depression, the Civic Music Association brought artists from all areas of Appalachia to Asheville. If anything, the Rhododendron Festival, begun in 1928, increased in size and scope. More local organizations participated in the Rhododendron Parade, and week-long activities attracted visitors from all over the South.

Yet Asheville's efforts failed and the Depression worsened. Nothing seemed to work. Ready for a good tourist year in 1933, local merchants saw travelers take inexpensive trips to the Chicago Fair. Sadly, the same thing happened in 1934. Hopeful that the new parkway and national park would lure both capital and tourism dollars into the economy, the city watched both projects bog down in New Deal red tape. Again ready for a big tourist season in 1935, infantile paralysis broke out in the South. Although Asheville had none, the season was ruined. "We were whipped," groaned Frank Coxe, "You couldn't do anything in Asheville anymore." For Asheville, little would be done until after World War II.

CHAPTER XI

Cool, Green Asheville

A boy tries his luck in Western North Carolina circa 1895. Fishing and hunting were favorite sports for mountaineers and tourists who came to the area in record numbers after 1880. Courtesy, J.H. Tarbell, North Carolina Collection, Pack Memorial Library

Asheville has been discovered many times in its past. The Cherokees came first, followed by explorers, traders, botanists, and settlers from the east who, stumbling across the Blue Ridge, found themselves in a veritable Garden of Eden waiting to be developed and exploited.

Asheville was also discovered in the 1920s by Floridians, by boomers and sooners, by speculators and second-home developers who hoped to make the city a "Miami north." Since the completion of the interstate highway system through the mountains in 1966, ever increasing numbers of summer people have returned to cool, green Asheville.

The picture of Asheville as a quaint, art-deco city set in the Garden of Eden is part of its current appeal, intentionally romanticized for summer people. One advertisement promoting a development in 1973 called Asheville an "Un-City; un-crowded, un-hurried, un-polluted," an unspoiled town in the cool, green mountains.

Since the 1890s, city government in Asheville has helped to maintain this image of "resort Asheville." Many of the city's civic improvements such as paving streets, building parks, planting trees, sponsoring a regional airport, constructing enormous civic centers and city halls, reflected efforts at beautification and progress designed to impress summer people more than natives.

A city of cabins and castles, Asheville has a history dominated by local mountaineers, shown here circa 1920, as well as by the rich and famous. Hardy and self-sufficient, the mountaineers depended on Asheville as a mercantile, banking, and government center. Courtesy, Ewart Ball Collection, Southern Highlands, UNC-Asheville

Also since the 1890s, Asheville's economy has fluctuated according to a boomer and sooner cycle. The booms of the 1880s, 1920s, and 1960s were followed by busts in 1893, 1930, and 1975, always with devastating social consequences. Gradually, Asheville became a city of palaces and shacks, of hotels and tenants, of the rich and the poor. If there was an Asheville of magnificent hotels, ramshackle boardinghouses, and health resorts there was also a town of immigrants living above stores around Pack Square, of blacks squeezed into shacks, and of mountaineers pressed together in mobile home parks on the city's outskirts. For every model development that smacked of English manors and estates there was a "Dixon town" clustered behind Pack Square along Valley and Eagle streets.

Asheville's legacy as a resort town has served to alienate many in Buncombe County. Remembering the city's extravagant building programs of the 1920s and subsequent indebtedness that cost them added taxes, a considerable number of county residents have come to distrust, even openly oppose, Asheville's pretentions as "the queen city of the mountains." Indeed, politicians from Buncombe County have for four decades sought election to local offices on the single issue of opposition to any of Asheville's plans for annexation, consolidation, or cooperation with the county.

The tension between the city and county has lessened somewhat in the 1980s, but it is still a divisive issue. Since the Appalachian Regional Development Act of 1965, much of Asheville's progress has come through its designation as a growth center for Western North Carolina. Improvements in the Appalachian interstate highway system, the location of federal and state agencies in Asheville, the millions of dollars in grants for urban development and improved health care all had the net effect of encouraging the movement of locals from outlying areas into the city and county.

Instead of moving into the city itself however, mountaineers settled in strip developments along the new highways south, west, and east of the city. Discouraged by restrictive housing codes, by higher taxes, and by a city government they perceived as unsympathetic, natives from surrounding counties preferred to live in mill towns such as Swannanoa and Enke. For them, Asheville was a great place to shop and visit, but not to live.

Asheville's continued resolve to remain a tourist, convention, and re-

Top: *Harvey Firestone's Ford Tri-Motor Plane is pictured here at Baird's Bottom in North Asheville. Baird's Bottom is now Beaver Lake, created when Beaver Creek was dammed by a real estate development company. Courtesy, Ewart Ball Collection, Southern Highlands, UNC-Asheville*

Above: *Members of the Asheville Community Theatre pose on the Beaver Lake bridge in 1951. Bret Hart and Charlton Heston were early directors of the theatre. The group's popularity and reputation spread quickly after the 1950s. Courtesy, Ewart Ball Collection, Southern Highlands, UNC-Asheville*

sort town has mortgaged its future as well as its past. At the turn of the century, for example, the city's fathers determined to build a civic center near the old Battery Park Hotel. In order to insure the success of the new center, Asheville used its municipal authority to shut down several thriving businesses, including the old opera house, another small theatre, and two private museums. Except in private homes and resort hotels, there was little entertainment left in downtown Asheville by 1911. Few entertainment events were scheduled outside the civic center and Asheville, as a center for festivals, carnivals, theatricals, grand balls, concerts, performances, and dances, has never recovered.

Asheville's future affects the region as a whole. As early as 1885, the city moved to help establish an Appalachian national park. Fifty years later, it became the Great Smoky Mountain National Park. Ashevillians promoted good roads movements throughout Western North Carolina from the turnpikes of the 1820s to the interstates of today. The concept of a parkway running through the Blue Ridge Mountains partially grew out of relief programs in Asheville in 1931, and the city led in the construction of a regional airport on the Henderson-Buncombe County line. Famous as a watering place for South Carolinians as early as 1824, Asheville has had leaders from Edward Aston to Ken Michalove who have nourished the city's reputation as a health center. Today, the magnificent facilities at St. Joseph's and Memorial Mission hospitals together with the Mountain Area Health Education Center testify to a century-old resolve.

Lastly, it seems that Asheville has discovered itself. As a city that is now almost 200 years old, Asheville is no longer the undiscovered Garden of Eden it once was. From the Western North Carolina Historical Association housed in the Smith-McDowell Museum to the Asheville-Buncombe Preservation Society, there is renewed interest in Asheville's past, present, and future. The opening of Lexington Park, the construction of a new downtown hotel, and the renovation of Wall Street and South Pack Square all point to a new rebirth. The object is not to recapture the frenetic boom of the 1920s or the gossipy grandeur of the Victorian era, but, instead, to continue the past into the present.

The vigilance of preservation groups together with an increased appreciation of the city's past and a bright economic future promise to keep Asheville a pleasant place to live, no less in the future than in the fascinating past. You can go home again to Asheville, a city in the land of the sky.

The 600 acres of rhododendrons in Craggy Gardens comprise the largest accessible stand in the country. Photo by Cotter/Carol & Adrian Cotter

Facing page, top: *"Built not for the present alone, but for ages to come, and the admiration of generations yet unborn." E.W. Grove built his dream, the Grove Park Inn, in the mountains of Western North Carolina. In 1921 Walter M. Harris rendered the magnificent hotel in oils. Courtesy, Priscilla Ann Hendricks, Brevard, North Carolina*

Facing page, bottom, far left: *The Banquet Hall of the Biltmore Estate features sixteenth-century Flemish tapestries,* The Return from the Chase *carving above the fireplace by Karl Bitter, the Vanderbilt crest, eighteenth- and nineteenth-century Dutch and Spanish copper pieces, and statues of St. Joan of Arc and St. Louis by Bitter. Courtesy, Biltmore House and Gardens Archives*

Facing page, bottom, left: *The library of George Vanderbilt in the Biltmore Estate contains over 20,000 books on art, landscaping, architecture, history, and classical novels. The room also features carvings by Karl Bitter, a seventeenth-century French tapestry, and the ceiling painting by Giovanni Antonio Pellegrini. Courtesy, Biltmore House and Gardens Archives*

The Biltmore Estate now occupies about 8,000 acres. Opened to the public in 1930 by Cornelia Vanderbilt Cecil and her husband, the estate is still in the Vanderbilt family and visited by thousands each year. Courtesy, Biltmore House and Gardens Archives

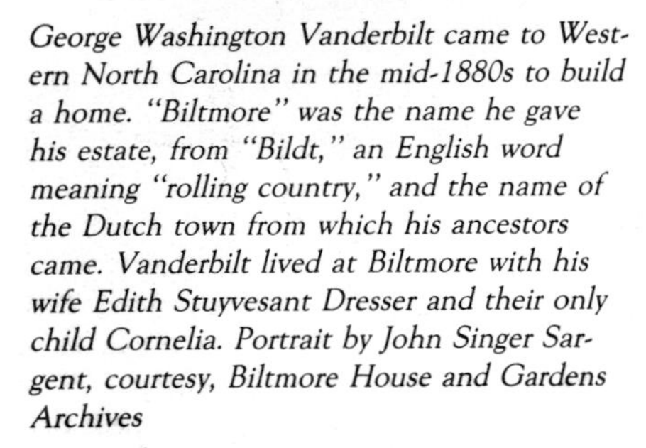

George Washington Vanderbilt came to Western North Carolina in the mid-1880s to build a home. "Biltmore" was the name he gave his estate, from "Bildt," an English word meaning "rolling country," and the name of the Dutch town from which his ancestors came. Vanderbilt lived at Biltmore with his wife Edith Stuyvesant Dresser and their only child Cornelia. Portrait by John Singer Sargent, courtesy, Biltmore House and Gardens Archives

Edith Stuyvesant Dresser was "first lady" of the Biltmore Estate. Portrait by Boldini, courtesy, Biltmore House and Gardens Archives

Facing page, top, right: *Surrounded by family photographs, the boarders at the Old Kentucky Home would gather in the parlor to mingle, swap stories, and listen to Mabel Wolfe sing and play the piano. At one time in vaudeville, Mabel and a friend toured the South as the "Dixie Melodie Twins." Photograph by Susan Lanier*

Facing page, top, far right: *Julia Elizabeth Wolfe, Thomas Wolfe's mother, was a businesswoman ahead of her time. She not only operated a boardinghouse, but speculated in the real estate market in Western North Carolina and Florida. During the Depression Mrs. Wolfe lost almost all of her real estate, including the Old Kentucky Home. Although the bank auctioned her boardinghouse, she was allowed to continue to live there and rent out rooms. Photograph by Susan Lanier*

Facing page, bottom: *The dining room of the Old Kentucky Home served as the setting for many pages of Thomas Wolfe's* Look Homeward, Angel. *The painting was done in acrylics by Robert MacDonald Graham, Jr., from Greenwood, Missouri, during a visit to Asheville in the summer of 1979. Courtesy, Robert MacDonald Graham, Jr.*

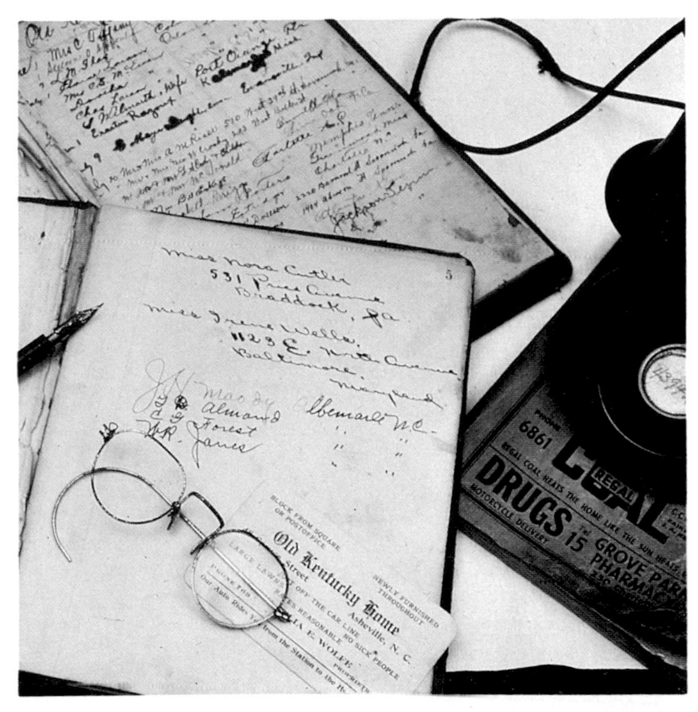
Miss Nora Cutler
Braddock, Pa.
Miss Irene Wells
Baltimore
Maryland
Albemarle N.C.
Old Kentucky Home
Asheville, N. C.
NEWLY FURNISHED THROUGHOUT
BLOCK FROM SQUARE OR POSTOFFICE
NO SICK PEOPLE
6861
REGAL COAL HEATS THE HOME LIKE THE SUN HEATS
DRUGS
15
GROVE PARK
PHARMACY
MOTOCYCLE DELIVERY

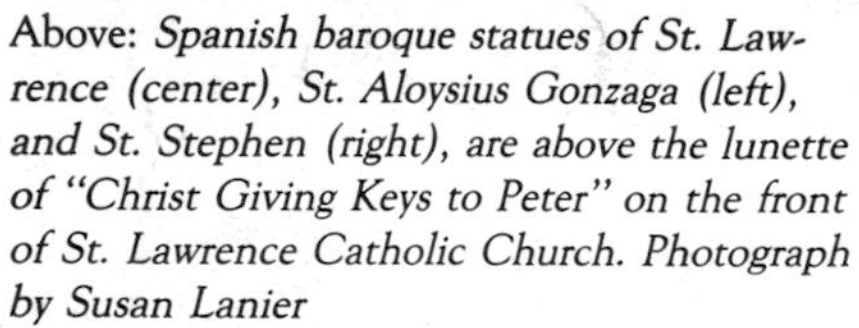

Above: *Spanish baroque statues of St. Lawrence (center), St. Aloysius Gonzaga (left), and St. Stephen (right), are above the lunette of "Christ Giving Keys to Peter" on the front of St. Lawrence Catholic Church. Photograph by Susan Lanier*

Top, right: *The spring house and wash pots at the Vance Birthplace evoke a rural Asheville of another era. Photograph by Susan Lanier*

Bottom, right: *Produce is not the only thing sold at the Western North Carolina Farmers' Market. Dried flowers, cured hams, stone-ground flours and meals, handmade crafts and furniture, and even Christmas trees and wreaths can be purchased in the market. Photograph by Susan Lanier*

Facing page, top: *Asheville glimmers in this view from Sunset Mountain. Photograph by Susan Lanier*

Facing page, bottom, right: *A drive through Asheville's fall foliage reveals the beauty of "America's Eden." Photograph by Susan Lanier*

Facing page, bottom, far right: *The city seal is featured above a brass door in the City Building. Photo by Cotter/Carol & Adrian Cotter*

CITY OF ASHEVILLE
1797
1883
NORTH CAROLINA

N W BANK

CHAPTER XII

PARTNERS IN PROGRESS

Facing page: *The Asheville skyline is shown here from Beaucatcher Mountain to the east in the area near Beaucatcher Tunnel. It was from this vicinity on a summer evening in the late 1800s that Christian Reid and a group of friends commented that surely this is the "promised land . . . the land of the sky." Photo by Cotter/Carol & Adrian Cotter*

In its very early years Asheville was an assembly point and way station for vast flocks of turkeys herded on foot from the mountains of Western North Carolina and Tennessee to market in Charleston, South Carolina. If there are any particular human capabilities needed in driving large numbers of turkeys over long distances, they are patience and skill. Those two attributes have, over the decades, set the tone for Asheville's growth and development.

The city developed, fortunately, in a number of directions. It embraced textiles, but did not become a "textile town." It sprouted a few furniture plants, but did not become a "furniture town." Asheville has always retained the diversification necessary for economic stability.

In the rural areas in Buncombe County tobacco became the money crop. It still is to a large extent, but a turn to the production of other money crops such as tomatoes is beginning to be apparent.

Asheville became a magnet for people suffering from tuberculosis and other respiratory diseases. At the turn of the century the town was dotted with sanitariums, and caring for victims of the disease became a major industry. Today tuberculosis is treated differently, but the city's head start in health care helped make it a medical center for the entire seventeen-county Western North Carolina area.

Probably the most interesting and certainly one of the most durable industries to flourish in Asheville is that of tourism. The city is near the geographic center of one of the most visually appealing sections of the United States. It is also the headquarters for the Blue Ridge Parkway, a 450-mile-long national park.

Today the industrial mix of the community remains diversified. The previous emphasis on textiles and furniture is fading fast, but new manufacturing plants, some of them on the cutting edge of technology, are taking up the slack. These new businesses will help ensure a future for Asheville as rich as its past.

The organizations whose stories are detailed on the following pages have chosen to support this important literary and civic project. They illustrate the variety of ways in which individuals and their businesses have contributed to the city's growth and development. The civic involvement of Asheville's businesses, institutions of learning, and local government, in cooperation with its citizens, has made the community an excellent place to live and work.

WESTERN NORTH CAROLINA HISTORICAL ASSOCIATION

Dr. William E. Highsmith, former president, Western North Carolina Historical Association.

The Western North Carolina Historical Association is headquartered in the Smith-McDowell House, a recently restored Asheville residence.

The Western North Carolina Historical Association is one of the many organizations of its type that created its own home.

The association was founded in 1952 by a diverse group of historians, amateur and otherwise, residing in the far west counties of North Carolina.

The first president was Dean William E. Bird of Western Carolina University.

The original charter outlined the group's purposes as, "to preserve and encourage the study of the history of Western North Carolina, to collect historical materials, to foster historical study and writing, to present awards for historical work, to preserve sites, buildings, and objects of historical interest, to observe historic dates, and to sponsor tours of historic places."

And in its 34-year span, the association has done all of those and in good measure.

But mark the injunction, "to preserve sites, buildings, and objects. . . ." In that respect the group has excelled.

In 1973, through a series of fortunate events, the society learned of the historic background of the Smith-McDowell House, a gracious brick residence then slowly decaying on the fringe of Asheville.

The Smith-McDowell House was one of a very few pre-Civil War structures remaining in western North Carolina.

In 1974 the property on which the house was located was bought by the Asheville-Buncombe Technical College. The Western North Carolina Historical Association was able to lease the Smith-McDowell House from the college.

Then came seven years of planning, hard work, and actual restoration.

A committee headed by Mrs. Edward E. McDowell was appointed. Members included Lieutenant Colonel Frank Austin, Johnnie Baxter, Mrs. Joshua F.B. Camblos, Jack Cole, Dr. Francis Hulme, Mrs. Cromwell Murray, Henry Arch Nichols, and Mrs. Viola Stevens.

Mrs. Camblos spearheaded the fundraising effort and money was obtained from state, city, county, federal, and private sources.

Restoration was done in two phases. Exterior stabilization was begun in October 1977, and interior work started in May 1980. The house was ready for occupancy in February 1981.

Since then it has served as a headquarters for the Western North Carolina Historical Association and as a museum.

The Smith-McDowell Museum of Western North Carolina History is operated by a director and assistant director responsible to the board of Smith-McDowell Associates.

Efforts to restore the grounds of the house in accordance with a turn-of-the-century landscape plan developed for the property are now under way. The original plans were drawn by the firm of Frederick Law Olmsted, pioneer American landscape architect who designed Central Park in New York City and the Biltmore Estate in Asheville.

Smith-McDowell Associates has plans to enlarge and enhance the museum. They include the construction of a compatible carriage house that would increase exhibition and storage space and provide office space for the staff.

During the restoration years and subsequent operation as a headquarters-museum, the following people have served as president of the historical association: Jack Cole, Mrs. Joshua Camblos, Dr. Francis P. Hulme, Dr. Carl Ross, Dr. William E. Highsmith, and Dr. Gordon McKinney. The president now is Peter Mallett.

ST. JOSEPH'S HOSPITAL

St. Joseph's Hospital, 1985.

St. Joseph's Hospital, a general diagnostic, surgical, and acute care institution, serves as a regional medical center for western North Carolina. The hospital was founded in 1900 by the Sisters of Mercy of Belmont, who opened an 18-bed tuberculosis sanitorium in Asheville at 40 French Broad Avenue. Later the sanitorium was moved to 33 Starnes Avenue. In 1909 the Sisters purchased a building on a 22-acre site on Biltmore Avenue, the location of the present hospital. The building housed 20 beds.

A south wing to accommodate 35 patients went up in 1916. Eight years later an administration building and a north wing were completed, bringing the institution's capacity to 95 beds. St. Joseph's Sanitorium was converted to a general hospital in 1938 and its capacity was increased to 110 beds. That same year St. Joseph's Hospital Guild was started.

St. Joseph's now includes 283 patient care units, all private rooms with baths. It maintains a medical staff of more than 286 physicians representing every specialty and employs more than 900 people. In 1985 the institution treated approximately 13,000 inpatients and 13,000 outpatients.

The hospital is fully accredited. It provides intensive, coronary, and intermediate care units; a short-term acute psychiatric unit, a pediatric section with sleep-in accommodations for parents, eight fully equipped operating rooms, an outpatient surgery annex, a cardiology diagnostic laboratory, nuclear medicine, full-body tomography, ultrasound, a noninvasive vascular laboratory, and an emergency department staffed by physicians 24 hours a day.

St. Joseph's offers one of the most comprehensive sports medicine programs in western North Carolina. The program includes full screening and diagnostic services and rehabilitation services in conjunction with the hospital's fully equipped Health Promotion/Physical Fitness Center.

The institution also provides several community service programs. These include senior citizen discount meals in the hospital's cafeteria, a special discount Medicare outpatient services program, and Lifeline, a communication system for area residents who live alone and have medical problems.

A five-story ambulatory care center is scheduled for completion by fall 1986 and will increase the hospital's capacity to 331 beds. The center will provide a variety of medical services for people who do not need to be admitted as bed patients. It will house outpatient surgery, expanded physical and respiratory therapy departments, a clinical laboratory and emergency department, and new occupational and speech therapy services.

The institution still is owned by the Sisters of Mercy but is managed by a lay board of directors. It is a subsidiary of the St. Joseph's Health Services Corporation. St. Joseph's Hospital, a nonprofit, tax-supported institution, serves those in need regardless of religious belief, race, or economic status.

The building and some of the property on Biltmore Avenue purchased by the Sisters of Mercy in 1909 to house their growing hospital in Asheville.

SQUARE D COMPANY

In the spring of 1961 a band of Square D pioneers headed by John N. Daniel moved into the mountains of western North Carolina, took over a plant formerly owned by a flatware manufacturer, and prepared to go into business. The Square D Company, an international organization manufacturing equipment to control and distribute electricity, was in an expansion phase. A friendly labor market, excellent climate, and matchless scenery drew the corporation's attention to the Asheville area.

In short order 26 families from Square D facilities nationwide were relocated to Asheville. New employees were hired locally, and in July the Asheville plant of the Square D Company began manufacturing. It was the start of a relationship that for a quarter-century has proven to be of major benefit to both the firm and the Asheville community.

At the outset Square D employed approximately 100 people in one building with about 90,000 square feet of floor space. The company now uses 435,000 square feet of space in two large buildings that house approximately 1,100 employees. The growth of the firm's Asheville operation is indicative of the growth of the Square D Company overall.

The business began in Detroit in 1902 with a couple of entrepreneurs who thought there probably was a future for an industry related to this newfangled electricity everyone had started to use. They organized the McBride Manufacturing Co., got an order for 1,000 fuses, hired a couple of female workers, and never looked back.

Today the Square D Company has total sales of approximately $1.4 billion. It operates 43 factories in the United States and 22 manufacturing and assembly plants offshore. It operates international sales offices in 22 foreign countries and in Hong Kong. It maintains 15 sales offices in Canada alone. It is in every respect a major U.S. industry functioning on an international basis and offering a broad spectrum of electrical control and distribution equipment for almost every conceivable application.

Square D's Asheville plant No. 1 was originally located in a building that had previously housed a silverware factory.

Square D Company's Asheville plant No. 2 also houses a divisional headquarters for the corporation.

Along the way the Square D facility in Asheville has established itself solidly as an outstanding corporate citizen. The firm's employees and executives contribute both their time and money to various community organizations, including United Way, United Arts, and the Asheville YMCA.

The high visibility of the Square D plant in the Asheville community is convincing evidence of an enlightened, compassionate corporate approach to the problems of society. It demonstrates a willingness on the part of management to help provide solutions to those problems. It is a reflection, too, of the personality of John N. Daniel, the man who led Square D into the mountains of western North Carolina and who has remained in Asheville to become a much-liked, valuable part of the fabric of the city.

The Square D Company has undergone many changes in leadership, in locale, and in name since 1902. But no change was more significant than a decision made in 1915, when the firm, then known as the Detroit Fuse and Manufacturing Co., decided to stamp a boxy, square initial "D" on the covers of a new line of switches contained in sheet-metal boxes. The square D caught the fancy of electricians and other users, and soon the phrase "Square D" was used universally to describe both the company and its products. In 1917 the firm recognized success in the marketplace by officially adopting "Square D Company" as its corporate name.

THOMS REHABILITATION HOSPITAL, INC., OF WESTERN NORTH CAROLINA

Thoms Rehabilitation Hospital's administration building.

Thoms Rehabilitation Hospital was originally founded to treat crippled children. It still does. But now it also treats patients of all ages. It is a place where futures are restored, where damaged bodies and lives are put back together. In its 47-year history the hospital has become a fully accredited institution with beds for 80 inpatients and a staff of more than 200.

The hospital truly is a product of community concern. In 1938 the Asheville Rotary Club, the Junior League, and the late Dr. John T. Saunders, an orthopedic surgeon, joined forces to "serve the crippled children of North Carolina." The facility they founded originally was housed in All Souls' Episcopal Church in the Asheville suburb of Biltmore. In 1939 it moved to the present 33-acre site, also in Biltmore, opening with 12 patients. It then was called the Asheville Orthopedic Home.

During the tragic poliomyelitis outbreaks of the 1940s and 1950s the fledgling institution assumed more than its share of the burden. It was a central point for the treatment of North Carolina polio patients, caring for thousands of individuals. The load was so heavy that at times tents were set up on the hospital lawn.

The hospital expanded many times during its early years. The Gruver Wing was added to the original building in 1948, and in 1959 the Britt Wing was constructed. The Thoms Wing went up in 1970.

That same year the institution's name was changed to Orthopedic Hospital and Rehabilitation Center. A major development program produced construction of the Handi-Skills Building (a sheltered workshop), the Orthopedic School, the Partin Speech and Hearing Center, and a gymnasium with a 60-foot heated therapeutic pool.

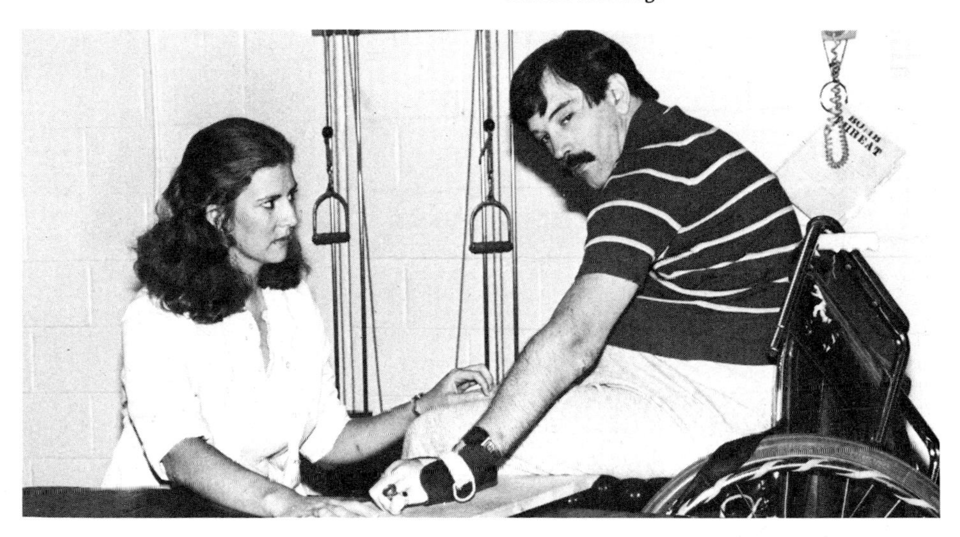

Physical therapist Margaret Balhoff works with patient Jim McCulley. Photo by Mollie Warlick

In 1976 the name of the institution was changed again. It became Thoms Rehabilitation Hospital, Inc., of Western North Carolina, honoring Harold Thoms, a major benefactor of the institution.

Probably more than any other person, Thoms left his mark on the institution. He contributed money and rallied community support. On at least one occasion he personally ran a backhoe to help construct the foundation of a new building. Today the hospital is an extension of Harold Thoms' generosity.

The latest building on the hospital campus, completed in 1986, is a $700,000 outpatient center. The 8,000-square-foot structure offers treatment areas; facilities for psychological care; and occupational, physical, and speech therapy departments. It also houses an auditorium for community health education services.

The hospital now offers a full range of clinical services and education; physical, occupational, and recreational therapy; vocational rehabilitation; a fully equipped laboratory, pharmacy, and X-ray department; speech/language pathology; audiology; social services; respiratory therapy; psychological counseling; and other programs. It cares for between 400 and 500 outpatients, and also provides special care units for spinal cord injuries, head injuries, and for stroke victims.

Thoms Rehabilitation Hospital's medical staff includes full-time licensed physicians who are specialists in physical medicine and rehabilitation, and who supervise the planning and implementation of the patients' treatment programs.

ASHEVILLE FEDERAL SAVINGS AND LOAN ASSOCIATION

The Asheville area's largest home-based financial institution is a child of the Great Depression.

Asheville Federal Savings and Loan Association was chartered on February 5, 1936. "It was a logical time to organize a savings and loan association," says William O. Prescott, now chief executive officer. "The country was beginning to emerge from the Depression. There were more jobs to be had and more money to be earned.

"Moreover, the creation in 1934 of the Federal Savings and Loan Corporation was sparking the development of savings and loan associations all over the United States.

"Equally important was the fact that there was a national hunger for homes. The Depression had hit hard at the home-building industry. For several years practically no new homes had been built anywhere. There was a pent-up demand for housing."

On Friday, February 21, 1936, a small ceremony was held in Room 207 of the Buncombe County Court House. At that time a set of by-laws for the new organization was adopted. Eight directors were elected. They were D.G. Florance, Dr. A.B. Greenwood, W. Randall Harris, Devere C. Lentz, Charles D. Parker, H. Edwin Pollock, Thomas C. Smith, and John W. Spicer.

They were, mostly, men who already had made names for themselves in the Asheville-Buncombe County community. They were also men who would continue to serve the community long after that night in a variety of ways. But it is doubtful that anything they did later had as marked and as permanent an impact on the community as the savings and loan association they put together that winter.

After the election Joe Holt of the Savings and Loan Division of the Federal Home Loan Bank office in Winston-Salem presented the charter. A few minutes later the first meeting of the board of directors was convened. The members elected Charles D. Parker, president; Thomas C. Smith, vice-president; and D.G. Florance, secretary/treasurer.

Temporary headquarters for the new association was established at 14 Church Street. The first savings and loan office was established at 12 Church Street.

The savings and loan office was opened for business on April 9, 1936. At the start a total of 711 shares at $100 each had been subscribed. "It may not seem like much now," Prescott says, "but in 1936 a respectable new home could be bought for $3,500."

The main office of Asheville Federal Savings and Loan Association is still on Church Street, where it opened for business in 1936.

Loans were made at 5.5 percent. The first dividends were 3 percent, paid semiannually. At the end of the first year of operation there were 206 subscribers with total paid shares of $159,651. Mortgage loans made totaled 77, and there were no delinquent accounts.

An informal history of the association written in 1980 by an employee notes: "In the early days of the association, history shows no evidence of discrimination. Mortgage loans were made to women as well as men, and at the first annual meeting Mrs. Ethel Lanford was appointed assistant secretary and authorized to sign checks."

Employees and executives of Asheville Federal Savings and Loan Association gathered for this photograph in 1971.

In the years that followed Asheville Federal Savings and Loan Association moved several times, but it never left Church Street. "It has never lost sight of its main purpose, either," says Prescott.

"Historically the savings and loan industry has provided funds so that people can buy homes. That always has been priority business at Asheville Federal Savings and Loan Association and will continue to be. We pride ourselves on being able to provide modern, innovative financing plans for modern home purchasers," he states.

That is not to say that there has been no change in the savings and loan industry.

"Deregulation of savings and loan associations and the entire financial services industry began in 1978." In the years 1980, 1981, 1982, and 1983, Congress continued to pass legislation removing curbs on the thrift industry. "Now Asheville Federal Savings and Loan Association offers its customers a full range of financial services," says Prescott.

The assets of Asheville Federal Savings and Loan Association now amount to $360 million, and the firm serves more than 62,000 accounts from its main office and 10 branch offices.

For more than 50 years the ways in which the organization serves the community have changed greatly. But it never has lost sight of the fact that it is essentially a device to help people build or buy homes.

MEMORIAL MISSION HOSPITAL

This rambling wooden building housed Asheville's Memorial Mission Hospital about the turn of the century. The hospital then was located at the intersection of Woodfin and Charlotte streets.

Take a good idea, give it to three determined mountain women, then add civic support, eons of volunteer effort, and 100 years of calendar time. The result, if lucky, could be something like Memorial Mission Hospital, a multimillion-dollar regional medical center serving seventeen western North Carolina counties and parts of three other states.

The founders were Anna Woodfin, Fanny Patton, and Rose Chapman. All three were active in the civic affairs of the small town of Asheville. In 1885 they decided that Asheville should have a hospital. They had at their disposal $10 and a five-room cottage. With that they started Flower Mission Hospital, the first hospital in the mountains and the second in the entire state of North Carolina.

They operated on the proverbial shoestring. A newspaper appeal produced furniture, and a local philanthropist came through with a handsome $100 donation. It was the beginning of a century of struggle, expansion, and progress as the hospital and its supporters battled to keep up with the needs of the community.

A turning point came in 1892, when the first structure designed and built in Asheville to house a hospital was opened. The new facility was named Mission Hospital. That year the institution's board put more than $7,000 into the building, leaving a year-end balance of $11.08 in cash.

In the years that followed, the hospital was expanded and later had to be rebuilt following a fire. A nursing school was also established.

Shortly after World War II, in response to a desperate need, a drive was begun to build a large general hospital in the community to replace a number of small, inadequately equipped general hospitals. An association was organized, funds were raised, and a consolidation took place. The result was Memorial Mission Hospital, formed by the merger of Mission Hospital, Biltmore Hospital, Victoria Hospital, and the Asheville Colored Hospital. Later the Aston Park Hospital was closed, leaving Memorial Mission and St. Joseph's as the only two general hospitals in the community.

In 1975 the Mountain Area Health Education Center, which trains general practitioners and other health professionals, was built adjacent to Memorial Mission. It was also the first hospital in western North Carolina to offer open-heart surgery, 24-hour emergency room coverage, a linear accelerator, and many other technological advances.

Development of Memorial Mission has been steady. Improvements in services, equipment, and techniques take place constantly. New buildings and new facilities appear regularly. The most recent is a new outpatient surgical unit, completed at a cost of $1.5 million for the building and $650,000 for equipment.

Memorial Mission Hospital is now a mature institution, offering the widest-possible range of modern health services. It is well positioned to meet the challenges of the future, and looks forward confidently to its second hundred years.

The Memorial Mission Hospital complex in 1986.

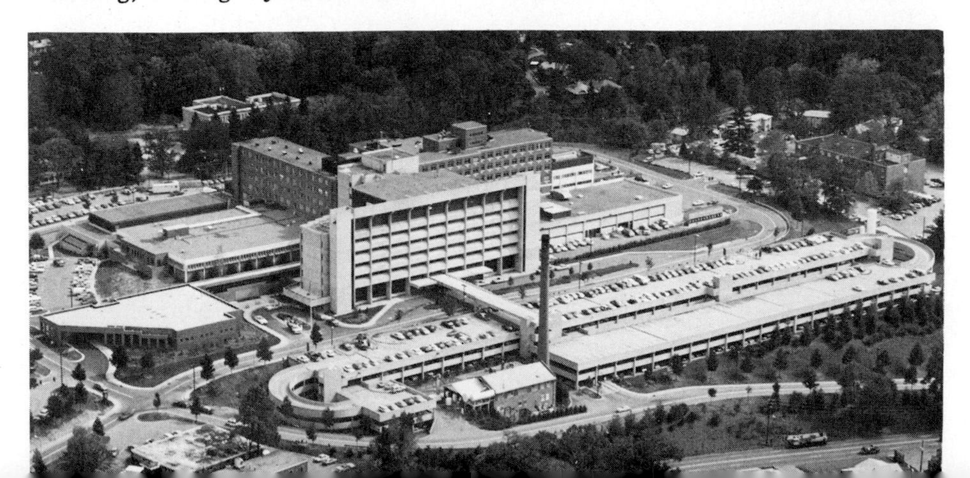

APPALACHIAN HALL

Appalachian Hall is situated on beautifully landscaped grounds overlooking the Swannanoa River Valley.

"Appalachian Hall is a community resource," says Dr. Alan Krueger. "We accept patients from anywhere, but our major function is to provide comparatively short-term care for acutely ill patients who come to us mostly from Asheville and Buncombe County and the surrounding area."

Dr. Krueger is medical director of the institution, a fully accredited 100-bed hospital for the treatment of mental illness. Appalachian Hall, licensed by the State of North Carolina, offers an adult psychiatric unit, an intensive services unit, a substance abuse treatment program called Woodhill, a child and adolescent treatment program, an outpatient service, and what Dr. Krueger calls a partial hospitalization program.

"The partial hospitalization program," says Dr. Krueger, "is but one example of our commitment to provide quality health care as effectively and efficiently as possible. Patients in this program have progressed to the point where it is no longer necessary or desirable for them to stay in the hospital 24 hours a day. They participate in the full therapeutic program but are allowed to go home at night, thus reducing the cost of care. This program illustrates the wide variety of therapeutic offerings which helps us keep pace with the changing health care needs of the 1980s."

The name "Appalachian Hall" is also firmly attached to the hospital building, a handsome, turn-of-the-century structure of vaguely Tudor style situated atop a ridge in the Asheville suburb of Kenilworth. The original Appalachian Hall—then called Kenilworth Inn—was built in 1890. It was made of wood with a stone entrance and was a popular resort hotel.

In 1909 the building was destroyed by fire. The owner began rebuilding the hotel in 1913 but ran into a scarcity of materials caused by the onset of World War I. Eventually the building was completed by the U.S. Army and converted into a hospital. The Army relinquished possession of the facility in 1922, when it again became a resort hotel.

The hotel folded in 1929, another victim of the Great Depression. Two years later the building was sold to two Asheville physicians who had been operating a hospital they called Appalachian Hall in a much smaller facility. Kenilworth Inn became Appalachian Hall.

Appalachian Hall provides a full-service program of recreation and therapy for the mentally ill.

And, except for World War II, when it was taken over by the U.S. Navy, it has remained a privately owned and operated facility for the treatment of mental illness.

The completely equipped Appalachian Hall is located on beautifully cared for grounds overlooking the Swannanoa River Valley. It offers a full array of recreational and therapeutic facilities. In 1978 the Asheville physicians who owned the hospital sold it to Psychiatric Institutes of America, a subsidiary of National Medical Enterprises.

SWANNANOA CLEANERS, INC.

Horse-drawn wagons were the mainstay of urban transportation when Swannanoa Cleaners, Inc., started in business in Asheville in 1900.

Swannanoa Cleaners, Inc., was founded in 1900 by Canie N. Brown in a small office on Church Street in midtown Asheville. Six employees took in the wash in what had been the First Christian Church building. Eighty-six years later the firm is still on the same spot. Its neighbors are the First Presbyterian and Central Methodist churches, proving that cleanliness is next to godliness.

Early home deliveries were made by horse and wagon. The trip to West Asheville over Carrier Bridge across the French Broad River took all day.

Moving into the horseless carriage years, Brown purchased one of the first automobiles in town, a 1905 Cadillac. Asheville's main streets were paved by this time, and the city was growing with the tourist trade. A fleet of 17 trucks replaced the horses, providing home delivery service.

The Roaring Twenties saw the company expand its retail and commercial laundry business. Even though the banks closed, somehow Swannanoa managed to survive the Great Depression.

In 1930 Bretney Smith, Sr., resigned from the T.C. Smith Wholesale Drug Company, which had been founded in 1869 by his grandfather, and walked across the street to join his father-in-law, Canie Brown, in the laundry business. He installed the Zoric Petroleum System of cleaning. Now Swannanoa was in the dry-cleaning business as well.

Steady growth occurred in the 1940s and 1950s, at which time a linen supply division was established.

Swannanoa became well known for its long-standing policy of fairness to its customers and concern for its employees. When a competitor was damaged by a fire, Swannanoa was there to help.

Following the death of Canie Brown at the age of 89 in 1963, Bretney Smith, Sr., assumed the presidency of Swannanoa and Bretney Smith, Jr., joined the firm.

This is one of six modern full-service plants operated in Asheville by Swannanoa Cleaners, Inc.

The next 10 years saw the establishment of four more full-service plants located north, south, east, and west on major thoroughfares leading into Asheville. Feeling that the retail market had been effectively covered, Swannanoa discontinued its truck routes. A store was opened in a small local shopping center, Arden Square, in 1985. The enthusiastic response from customers has prompted plans for future expansions into fast-growing areas.

In 1972 the Suede Life System of leather cleaning was introduced to the consumer suede and leather market. Also, a wholesale route and mail-order operation was begun, serving 200 dry-cleaning plants in Tennessee, Virginia, and North and South Carolina.

Following the death of Bretney Smith, Sr., in 1977, Bretney Smith, Jr., was elected president of Swannanoa. His son, Bretney, and daughter, Stacy, are both employed by the company, representing the fourth generation of continuous family management.

Swannanoa Cleaners specializes in supplying quality, all-cotton linens to fine restaurants, country clubs, and popular resorts. The firm also fulfills the exacting demands of the thriving health care and retirement communities of western North Carolina.

The future looks bright. A stable, experienced, and dedicated work force, coupled with aggressive marketing and management, should provide for a healthy company for years to come.

THE ASHEVILLE SCHOOL

An expectation of leadership is the foundation of The Asheville School. Its students are expected to play leadership roles while attending the institution and later in college. Asheville School graduates are expected to become decision-makers in American society.

And that expectation is realized with remarkable frequency. Asheville School graduates can be found in positions of leadership all across the cultural, business, and industrial reaches of the nation.

Mitchell Hall is the main building on the campus of The Asheville School.

The Walker Arts Center on Asheville School's campus is both an art gallery and a completely equipped center for the performing arts.

The institution enjoys a strong and positive relationship with the Asheville community, but its students are drawn from all over the United States as well as from abroad. Its graduates have amassed an outstanding record of service to their communities, to their country, and to the world.

The Asheville School is the creation of two Ohioans—Newton Mitchell Anderson and Charles Andrews Mitchell. The pair were experienced educators and had pioneered in progressive approaches to education. Both wanted to create a high-caliber school for boys away from the distractions of a big city.

In 1900 Anderson and Mitchell founded The Asheville School in a combined classroom-dormitory they designed and built on a 750-acre tract of land on the western fringe of Asheville, then a small town. In addition, they recruited a fine corps of faculty members. Fifty boys, half of them grammar school students, were enrolled that first year. Anderson and Mitchell served as co-headmasters. The school, based on sound principles and helped by what was then thought to be, with some accuracy, "the healthiest climate in the world," grew steadily, but it was not without financial problems.

In 1926 a financially beset Anderson sold The Asheville School to a Pittsburgh resident who changed the name of the institution to The Asheville School for Training in Christian Leadership and also began to change the institution itself. In 1933, in the midst of the Depression, an alumni group headed by trustee chairman Philip R. Clarke and headmaster Howard Bement raised $350,000, bought the school, and set it back on course.

As the years passed, The Asheville School admitted day students, erected needed buildings, developed broad-range athletic and cultural programs, and saw second- and third-generation students appear on the campus. In 1971, 17 girls were accepted as day students. A new dormitory to accommodate female boarding students is planned for the future.

John L. Tyrer has been headmaster of the school since 1964. In 1986 enrollment in four grades, called forms, stood at 201 students, all of whom are being prepared academically to sustain that expectation of leadership, the hallmark of The Asheville School.

THE GROVE PARK INN AND COUNTRY CLUB

The Grove Park Inn, when it originally opened in 1913, looked much like it is shown here. This is the west face of the original building overlooking the golf course.

"Build not for the present alone, but for ages to come, and the admiration of generations yet unborn." This was the dream of Edwin Wiley Grove (1850-1927) of Tennessee, owner of a pharmaceutical firm in St. Louis that produced Grove's Bromo-Quinine and Grove's Tasteless Chill Tonic. He came to Asheville as a summer resident and found the climate so beneficial to his health that he bought land here, including a large acreage on Sunset Mountain. The idea of building a unique resort overlooking the mountains he had come to love soon became a reality. He consulted many architects, but none could grasp his idea, so he turned to Fred L. Seely, his son-in-law. Without an architect or a contractor, this remarkable man built an edifice that came to be known as the "finest resort hotel in the world."

The hotel was built of boulders taken from Sunset Mountain, hauled to the site by wagon trains, and fitted into place by Italian stonemasons and hundreds of local laborers. Built in 11 months and 27 days, the opening date was July 12, 1913, with William Jennings Bryan delivering the official address. The lobby, or "Great Hall," 120 feet long and 80 feet wide, was constructed with elevators running through the chimney rockwork and massive fireplaces large enough to burn 12-foot logs. A superb orchestral organ, with 7,000 pipes, was built by Ernest Skinner of Boston especially for the inn.

Edwin Grove leased his hotel from 1914 to 1927 to his manager, Fred Seely, whose policies, though

Grove Park Inn general manager Herman - R. von Treskow directed the hotel's recent $25-million expansion program. Courtesy, Asheville Citizen-Times

appreciated by his select conservative clientele at the time, would seem a bit austere now. Children were discouraged; pets forbidden; only low tones and whispers were permitted after 10:30 p.m.; and no slamming of doors. As the hotel literature states, this was all necessary "to maintain a place where tired, busy people may get away from all annoyances and rest their nerves." Many famous names appeared on the early guest registers: Thomas Edison, Harvey Firestone, Henry Ford, Woodrow Wilson, Calvin Coolidge, the Rockefellers, Enrico Caruso, Bela Bartok, the Roosevelts, General Eisenhower, and F. Scott Fitzgerald.

During World War II the inn was leased by the U.S. government. In 1942 Axis diplomats and consular officials were interned here while awaiting repatriation. Though completely cut off from the outside world, they were treated as ordinary guests, paying their own expenses. In 1944-1945 the hotel was part of an Army redistribution station where soldiers back from overseas service rested and relaxed before being reassigned to further duty.

The inn became part of the Jack Tar Hotel chain in 1955. Two modern wings were added in 1958 and 1964, and in 1976 the adjoining Country Club of Asheville, with its 18-hole golf course, swimming pool, and historic clubhouse, was purchased. The inn was listed on the National Register of Historic Places in 1973.

A new era began in 1982, when general manager Herman - R. von Treskow announced a multimillion-dollar renovation and expansion program. In the spring of 1984 the first phase was completed. With the renovation of the main inn and the addition of a new conference center (the Sammons Wing), the once-seasonal resort opened year-round. The second phase, completed in 1985, involved the renovation of the country club for conferences and social functions, and the addition of horse-drawn carriage rides and a children's playground. In 1986 a major indoor sports complex was completed.

Edwin Grove's dream has become a reality. Now completely restored and expanded, The Grove Park Inn and Country Club is ready for the twenty-first century and the "admiration of generations yet unborn."

Rides in an antique horse-drawn buggy are reminiscent of the lasting charm of early days at The Grove Park Inn and Country Club. Courtesy, Asheville Citizen-Times

In 1984 the historic main inn was completely restored, and the 204-bed Sammons Wing (at right) was added.

PEPSI-COLA BOTTLING CO. OF ASHEVILLE INC.

It was a great idea in 1898. It was a great idea in 1936. And it is still a great idea in 1986.

The great idea was Pepsi-Cola and it occurred first to a pharmacist named Caleb Bradham in the eastern Carolina city of New Bern. Bradham was 31 years old at the time, and, like many pharmacists of the era, he enjoyed experimenting with soda fountain drinks.

One day Bradham produced a mixture of spices, juices, and syrups that seemed just right. He tried it on his customers. They liked it and called it "Brad's Drink." But Bradham called it "Pepsi-Cola," and that name stuck.

This modern plant, located in the Sweeten Creek Road Industrial Park, is the home of the Pepsi-Cola Bottling Co. of Asheville Inc. Courtesy, Asheville Citizen-Times

In 1902 Bradham founded the Pepsi-Cola Co. in the back room of his pharmacy. He began by making syrup to be mixed and sold at soda fountains, but soon branched into bottling the drink himself.

In 1903 the Pepsi-Cola name became a registered trademark, and Bradham began to build a network of distributors. The company changed hands several times during the sugar shortage of World War I, finally being taken over by a major candy manufacturer. However, the firm prospered, and was able to survive both the Depression and World War II. Pepsi-Cola is now manufactured in 145 countries including the Soviet Union and the People's Republic of China. Today the Pepsi-Cola Co. is a subsidiary of Pepsico, Inc., a holding company.

John Teeter, general manager of the Pepsi-Cola Bottling Co. of Asheville Inc.

The history of what is now the Pepsi-Cola Bottling Co. of Asheville began in 1925, when Lee P. Frans, a secretary in a Winston-Salem tobacco company office, decided to go into business for himself. He then moved his family to Hickory and acquired the Orange Crush bottling plant there.

Frans worked hard, and his business grew. In 1936 he was persuaded to take on a franchise to manufacture and bottle Pepsi-Cola in the Hickory area.

In 1937 Pepsi-Cola entered the soft drink market in Hickory with a clear-glass 12-ounce bottle. At first Frans simply placed a few cases of Pepsi on each of his Orange Crush delivery trucks. However, by 1940 Orange Crush was almost a sideline, and Frans' company was in the Pepsi-Cola business. He soon found it necessary to add more trucks and expand his plant. In 1949 Frans acquired the Pepsi franchise in Spruce Pine, and one of his daughters and her husband were assigned to manage that facility. In 1925 the name of the firm became the Pepsi-Cola Bottling Co. of Hickory.

In May 1969 the Hickory franchise purchased the Pepsi-Cola Bottling Co. of Asheville. Another of Frans' sons-in-law, J. Lee Teeter, was brought in to head the operation. Along with the Asheville franchise, the buyers acquired the Asheville firm's plant on Swannanoa River Road. In 1976 the Pepsi-Cola Bottling Co. of Asheville built a modern distribution center in the Sweeten Creek Industrial Park.

John Teeter, a grandson of the founder of the Pepsi-Cola Bottling Co. of Hickory, is the general manager of the Asheville plant. In 1985 the Pepsi-Cola Bottling Co. of Asheville sold approximately 2.5 million cases of Pepsi, proving that it's still a great idea.

The Pepsi-Cola Bottling Co. of Hickory, where the parent company of the Asheville Pepsi-Cola bottling company got its start. The photo was taken in the mid-1930s. Courtesy, Asheville Citizen-Times

VAN WINKLE, BUCK, WALL, STARNES AND DAVIS, P.A.

Above: Kingsland Van Winkle. Courtesy, Asheville Citizen-Journal

Left: Thomas J. Harkins. Courtesy, Asheville Citizen-Times

"We were among the first ground-floor lawyers in Asheville," says O.E. Starnes with a grin. "Before that time Asheville lawyers had their offices on the upper floors of the buildings they occupied. They left the ground floors to the merchants who, the lawyers said, made more money."

The "we" refers to the law firm of Van Winkle, Buck, Wall, Starnes and Davis, P.A. In 1952 the firm moved from the Jackson Building on Pack Square into its own building at 18 Church Street where various tenants, including an early bicycle shop, had previously been located. In the fall of 1986 the firm moved to new, larger, renovated offices at 11 North Market Street, the only remaining brick street in town.

Law firm, 1986.

Kingsland Van Winkle, one of the firm's founding partners, came to Asheville about the turn of the century. Part of his early law practice was examining real estate titles for George W. Vanderbilt, who was then acquiring acreage for the now-famous Biltmore Estate.

Thomas J. Harkins, the other original partner, had earlier moved from Buncombe County to Oklahoma for health reasons. There he was elected to the territorial legislature and helped guide Oklahoma to statehood. Health restored, he returned to Asheville in 1907 to join forces with Van Winkle and found the firm that still carries the Van Winkle name. The two lawyers prospered over the years; in 1931 the firm became one of the largest then in Asheville when Kester Walton and Charles G. Buck, trial and real estate specialists, were added to it.

The name and constituency of the firm has undergone permutation over the decades as new lawyers came and others retired or answered the call to a higher court.

Robertson Wall and Buck, both retired, remain consultants to the firm. The active lawyers now with the firm, representative of many law schools and an impressive variety of regions, are listed in order of senority: Starnes; Roy W. Davis, Jr.; Brian F.D. Lavelle; Larry McDevitt; Philip J. Smith; Barry B. Kempson; Albert L. Sneed; Russell P. Brannon; Alfred J. Adams; Robert H. Haggard; Marla Tugwell; Shelley M. Pew; Allan R. Tarleton; Larry C. Harris, Jr.; Susan Strayhorn Barbour; Elizabeth M. Bryant; J. Hayden Harrell; and Michelle Rippon.

Harkins, an excellent trial lawyer, served as United States Attorney. "Van Winkle was an austere, imposing man, very proper, with a penchant for wing collars even into the 1960s," says Starnes. Van Winkle served as president of the North Carolina Bar Association, for many years as chairman of the State Board of Law Examiners, and as chancellor of the local Episcopal Diocese. Buck was also a chairman of the State Board of Law Examiners. These early partners established the firm's abiding tradition of public service. Consistent with its tradition of public service, the firm has supplied six presidents to the local District Bar, six governors and many committee chairmen to the North Carolina Bar Association, city and county attorneys, and a state senator. McDevitt recently concluded service as mayor of Asheville. Davis is the incumbent president of the North Carolina State Bar.

Van Winkle, Buck, Wall, Starnes and Davis, P.A., serves clients in most active fields of practice including corporate, tax, probate, and real estate law as well as insurance and general litigation. It is a stable, competent firm, some might also say conservative, but not too conservative to enjoy a chuckle about itself for being an Asheville pioneer of "ground-floor attorneys" that will soon move to new quarters "three flights up."

HIGHLAND HOSPITAL

Rumbough House, a turn-of-the-century mansion lovingly restored, is the administration building for Highland Hospital.

A transplanted Pennsylvanian who believed that the treatment of mental illness should involve treatment of the whole person was the founder of Highland Hospital, the oldest private psychiatric facility in the Southeast.

In 1904 Dr. Robert S. Carroll established a sanitarium in a small rented building in downtown Asheville. It was called the Halthenon, and it was devoted to the treatment of "mental, nervous, and habit disorders."

The location was no accident. Dr. Carroll settled down only after a nationwide search for the right place for his hospital. "Nature was prodigal with her bounty when she formed this natural park," he wrote. The park, of course, was Asheville.

But the downtown location was not satisfactory. In 1906 Dr. Carroll bought a farm on Zillicoa Street in the Montford neighborhood. By 1912 he had erected a 30-bed institution called Highland Hospital. He later acquired a 60-acre park surrounding the facility and a 400-acre tract of land on a nearby mountainside.

The land was put to good use. At a time when mental patients, for the most part, were kept in seclusion, Dr. Carroll pioneered in the treatment of the whole person. His patients hiked, worked in the garden, and got plenty of fresh air and exercise. He opposed the use of nicotine, alcohol, caffeine, and strong drugs. His patients ate a diet of fish, fowl, eggs, dairy products, and fresh vegetables. And they received unstinting, professional nursing care.

Dr. Carroll's regimen worked as well as any treatment plan of that period, probably a little better. Highland became well-known throughout the country.

As science began to unknot the puzzle of mental illness, Dr. Carroll was quick to adopt new techniques and treatments. He introduced innovations such as occupational therapy, arts and crafts, music, and recreational therapy. He kept the hospital in the forefront of developments in the field of psychiatry.

In 1939, anticipating retirement, Dr. Carroll donated the hospital to Duke University. However, he stayed on at the facility until his retirement in 1946.

Highland Hospital was continually expanded. In 1948 the facility suffered a tragic fire in which nine patients died. One was Zelda Fitzgerald, wife of writer F. Scott Fitzgerald. However, that setback was only temporary.

In 1981 a group of physicians affiliated with the institution, in conjunction with Psychiatric Institutes of America, Inc. (now a division of National Medical Enterprises, Inc.), bought the facility from Duke. It is a fully accredited 125-bed intermediate to long-term hospital offering a broad spectrum of services to treat all types of mental disorders. Special programs are offered for both adults and adolescents.

Dr. Jack W. Bonner III, medical director, heads a staff of approximately 230. Psychiatrists, clinical psychologists, social workers, nurses, activity therapists, and teachers work as a team to help their patients. Highland Hospital has experienced over 80 years of progress, but it still honors Dr. Carroll's concern for "the whole person."

Music in a relaxed social setting is part of therapy. Photo by Warner Photography

ROYAL CROWN BOTTLING CO. OF ASHEVILLE, INC.

The soft drink bottling business traditionally is a family affair, and Thomas H. Lamb, president of Royal Crown Bottling Co. of Asheville, Inc., is an example of that tradition. "I just grew up in this business," he says. "I was always around the plant, even as a child, doing something."

Lamb's company can be traced back to the Haskell Bottling Works, which, around the turn of the century, bottled and sold soda water in Asheville. In 1919 the Haskell Bottling Works was purchased by Chester Brown, who later acquired the local franchise for Nehi flavors. In 1936 Nehi bought out Royal Crown Cola. "That put us into the Royal Crown business," Lamb says.

Lamb's father, Hugh, went to work for Brown at the bottling company in 1925. Twenty-two years later, after World War II, Hugh Lamb and a partner, Elbert Lyman, bought the business from Brown.

Meanwhile, Thomas Lamb was graduated from Davidson College, served in the Armed Forces during the Korean Conflict, and worked for a time for an auto finance company. However, in 1959, at the age of 30, he went back to where he started and joined his father at the bottling company. Thomas Lamb became president of the firm in 1976; his father died two years later.

The first uniformed soft drink truck drivers in Asheville are shown lined up in front of an old delivery truck in this picture taken in 1927.

Prominently displayed in the front office of the Asheville Royal Crown plant is a faded picture of a group of nattily clad men aligned in front of an old-style open truck. The man on the extreme left is Lamb's father. "That picture was made in 1931. We had the first uniformed drivers in the city," he recalls. "I can still remember seeing my father's leather puttees standing in his closet.

"In those days we bottled Royal Crown mostly in 10- and 12-ounce returnable bottles in wooden cases holding 24-bottles. Just this year [1986] we stopped using returnable containers entirely, and I have a big bottle-washing machine in the back that I don't use any more. Mostly we sell now in two-liter plastic containers, and the retailers we serve have changed from mom-and-pop grocery stores to huge supermarkets."

The Royal Crown Bottling Co. of Asheville, Inc., at 44 Southside Avenue.

Royal Crown Bottling Co. of Asheville serves a 13-county area stretching from McDowell County in the east to Macon County in the west, and as far to the northeast as Yancey and Mitchell counties. It operates 14 truck routes from Asheville and three additional routes from a warehouse in Bryson City.

Standing next to Thomas Lamb's father in that faded photograph of early Royal Crown drivers is Ray Young, who was employed in sales for the bottling company all his working life. "He's long since been retired," says Lamb, "but he still comes into the office almost every day. He goes to the bank for us and picks up the mail and helps out a little. He's 78 now, but that's not so old."

It's certainly not "so old" in a people-oriented sort of family business like Thomas Lamb's.

BEVERLY-HANKS AND ASSOCIATES

George W. Beverly, 1904-1984, founder.

It took far more than just an allergy to tobacco dust to create the largest full-service real estate agency in western North Carolina, but that's how the firm of Beverly-Hanks and Associates got its start.

George W. Beverly, Sr., originally came from Laurinburg, North Carolina, to Durham, where he was enrolled in an executive training program with a tobacco company. However, he soon discovered he was allergic to tobacco dust, which is inescapable in Durham. He was then transferred to Asheville and given the position of supervision of cigarette sales over a wide area in the western end of the state.

Later he met and married an Asheville woman and decided, as many others have, to make Asheville his home. In 1946 he left the tobacco firm and opened the Beverly Realty Co. in the Vanderbilt Hotel, now a public housing facility for the elderly.

The firm did well, and in 1961 Beverly was joined in the business by his son, George Jr., a graduate of Duke University who had been working in sales in Atlanta. Four years later the company moved out of the hotel and into an office in a building it had purchased at 16 Church Street. "That's when the business really started to take off," says George Jr.

The other half of Beverly-Hanks and Associates arrived in Asheville in the capacity of a public official. W. Neal Hanks, a graduate of the University of Southern Mississippi, came to Asheville in 1967 from Mobile, Alabama. He became planning director of the city of Asheville, in charge of planning, zoning, and urban redevelopment and of the city's fast-growing metropolitan housing program. In 1972 Hanks resigned his position with the city and opened a real estate office on Market Street. The following year he moved the business to Biltmore Village.

George W. Beverly, Jr.

In 1976 the Beverly Realty Co., with nine salesmen, and the Hanks firm, with eight salesmen, merged to form Beverly-Hanks and Associates. "We had become good friends and good competitors," says Beverly. "We respected each other as businessmen, and a merger seemed to be logical. We first talked about the prospect of a merger while we both were attending a real estate convention at Myrtle Beach."

The merger proved successful, and the company has grown steadily since it was formed. In its first year in business, the firm had sales totaling approximately $14 million. In 1985 sales totaled $57.2 million. "That was an excellent year," says Hanks. "But we did well even during the so-called recession years of 1980, 1981, and 1982."

Now housed in a modern building opened in June 1976 and specifically designed for use as a real estate agency, Beverly-Hanks and Associates employs 50 people in sales and management with a sup-

W. Neal Hanks

port staff of eight. The building is located in downtown Asheville in one of the city's first urban-renewal areas, on a spot once occupied by a junior high school.

In 1983 the firm opened a second office on Hendersonville Road in the South Asheville suburbs. Two years later a third office was opened in Hendersonville, a predominately residential community 20 miles from Asheville.

Beverly-Hanks and Associates deals in residential, commercial, and industrial properties. It manages and rents property and is a major developer in the area. "We enjoy a sort of 'carriage trade' in selling residential property," states Beverly. "Our average residential sale is about $90,000."

The firm probably has made as big a mark on the community in its time as Edwin Wiley Grove, the patent medicine king who built many memorable structures in Asheville, did during his time. Over the years the firm planned, developed, and built such top-drawer residential areas as Oak Forest, Happy Valley, and Botany Woods, on the east side of Asheville. It also developed the Beverly Apartments, a large complex in South Asheville now transformed into condominiums. And it developed Executive Park, a five-building downtown office complex on urban-renewal land, adjacent to the firm's office.

"And we have helped bring some large industries into the community," Beverly says. "We assisted in the development and construction of new plants for such firms as Westinghouse, Reliance Electric, RCA, Switzer, and many others."

Both Beverly and Hanks are involved in work for the betterment of the community, but they prefer to talk about business—specifically the future of their business. "Asheville is just beginning to grow," says Hanks. "This town possesses more livability than any other comparably sized city on the Eastern Seaboard. The future for this beautiful area is truly unlimited."

The Beverly-Hanks and Associates headquarters at 300 Executive Park, Asheville.

BASF CORPORATION FIBERS DIVISION

History was made on December 16, 1985, when the Badische Corporation of Williamsburg, Virginia, purchased the assets of one of Buncombe County's oldest and largest industries, the American Enka Company. On January 1, 1986, the fiber operations of Badische and American Enka became known as the BASF Corporation Fibers Division. The parent firm, BASF of West Germany, is one of the world's largest chemical companies.

BASF Corporation Fibers Division has more than 7,500 employees and eight major manufacturing sites in the United States and Canada. Its products cover a broad range of fibers and yarns, including nylon, polyester, rayon, and acrylic used in carpeting, home furnishings, apparel, and hosiery, as well as in nonwoven and industrial products.

The division headquarters in Williamsburg includes administrative and marketing functions and carpet technical service operations. Central research, central engineering, and the textile fiber technical service operations are concentrated in Enka, North Carolina, along with the Enka nylon plant, which produces nylon yarns for carpets.

The history of American Enka dates back to 1928, when the Netherlands Artificial Silk Company of Arnhem, Holland, purchased about 2,200 acres of farmland located seven miles west of Asheville in Hominy Valley. After looking at more than 50 locations in the United States, the Dutch company selected the area because of its accessibility to raw materials and markets, ideal climate, good water supply, and readily available labor force. Here the Dutch built their first U.S. plant to produce viscose rayon yarns and open the North American market for rayon products.

These women in Dutch costumes were in front of the American Enka plant (now BASF Corporation Fibers Division) shortly after the 1929 opening in the Asheville suburb of Enka.

The bed of Hominy Creek was changed to circle the plant site, and a large area was flooded to create a reservoir. Along with the plant, the Dutch built a cafeteria, library, clubhouse, retail store buildings, post office, and village with homes for workers. A Dutch school was established in a nearby farmhouse.

The first yarn was spun on July 1, 1929, and the Hominy Valley became one of the nation's leading rayon centers, known for the high quality of its product. The company grew steadily, building additional rayon plants in East Tennessee at Lowland.

A nylon staple plant was completed at Enka in 1954, and later the more popular nylon filament yarn replaced the staple fiber. The following year a modern research center was completed at Enka. In 1958 the nylon facilities were expanded, and Enka manufactured a wide range of nylon products.

The company enjoyed its greatest period of growth during the 1960s. Both the research center and nylon plant were expanded, and a nylon plant was erected at Lowland. In 1965 the company entered the polyester yarn and staple markets. Four years later construction began on a nylon plant at Clemson, South Carolina. In 1972 a polyester filament plant was completed at Clemson.

While the Enka name forever will be ingrained in the community, the fibers operation at the plant moves forward into the twenty-first century as BASF—itself a proud logo, signifying more than 120 years of progress and innovation.

The BASF Corporation Fibers Division plant in the mountains of western North Carolina.

THE ASHEVILLE CITIZEN-TIMES PUBLISHING CO.

When Randolph Abbott Shotwell arrived in Asheville early in 1870 to become editor of a "bold, outspoken" newspaper, he had five dollars in his pocket.

When he left six months later he had $2.50. His sojourn in the mountains was not profitable, but it didn't lack for excitement. Shotwell was, indeed, a bold, outspoken editor, and he was forced to survive scuffles, sparring matches, and a shooting affray or two with infuriated readers.

His stay was short, but it made an indelible impression on the community. He left behind a newspaper called *The North Carolina Citizen,* a publication that was destined to outlive both Shotwell and the passions that made his tenure in the area lively.

Through the process of merger and permutation familiar to the newspaper publishing business, *The North Carolina Citizen* became *The Asheville Citizen,* a morning newspaper. *The Citizen* is one of the two feet on which The Asheville Citizen-Times Publishing Co. is firmly planted.

The other half of the combination is *The Asheville Times,* an afternoon publication. During the decades after 1860 the two newspapers were published in various places in downtown Asheville, at first separately, then, after a consolidation in 1930, together.

On January 1, 1939, the two newspapers moved into a new facility at 14 O. Henry Avenue. The building was designed by Anthony Lord, a noted Asheville architect. It was the first time either publication had operated in a plant expressly designed for publishing newspapers.

In 1953 the papers were acquired by the Peace family of Greenville, South Carolina. Later The Asheville Citizen-Times Publishing Co. was one of the three founding partners of Multimedia, Inc. Today Multimedia, Inc., has revenues of $335 million and operates TV and radio stations, newspapers, and cable television franchises, and also syndicates TV programming.

Still under construction is the new Asheville Citizen-Times *pressroom and mail room facility on Sardis Road in the Enka area west of Asheville.*

Editorial and administrative functions will continue to be performed in the existing Citizen-Times *plant at 14 O. Henry Avenue in downtown Asheville.*

The Asheville Citizen-Times Publishing Co. still is located on O. Henry Avenue and will be for the forseeable future. But at a site near Sardis Road in the suburb of Enka, the firm is erecting what amounts to a giant leap into the future.

The new building will consist of a pressroom, paper-storage area, and mail room facility. It also will house a M.A.N.-Roland Colorman 75 double-width offset press. The new press will offer *Citizen-Times* editors previously unknown flexibility in the use of color. It will offer readers clear, vibrant four-color illustrations and sharp, distinctive black-and-white photographs.

The *Citizen-Times* editorial, advertising, and administrative departments will remain in the downtown building. Page production will continue in the older facility to the point at which camera-ready paper pages are produced. Images of those pages will then be transmitted electronically from the plant on O. Henry Avenue to the new press facility in Enka. There aluminum plates will be produced and locked onto the press.

The plant at Enka will include a spacious mail room equipped with the most modern mail-handling machinery available. In addition, it will house a 75-day supply of newsprint, thus easing the mechanical problems involved in delivering newsprint to the press and taking printed newspapers away to subscribers through cramped downtown streets.

The new facility, built and equipped at a cost of more than $10 million, is a concrete expression of the confidence the managers of The Asheville Citizen-Times Publishing Co. have in the future of western North Carolina.

DANIELS BUSINESS SERVICES, INC.

Daniels Business Services, Inc., got its start on a bench in Pritchard Park in 1948. It has since gone on to become a major supplier of a wide array of communications services to Asheville area businesses.

In 1947 Ernest W. Daniels came to Asheville from Florida, a victim of tuberculosis. He fully expected to die there. But the Asheville climate and Daniels' own gritty determination to survive delayed the inevitable for 17 years.

Upon his arrival in Asheville, Daniels had to struggle to make a living. He was an expert typist and skilled in office procedures, and for a while he worked from a Pritchard Park bench, canvassing the offices around the park for typing jobs.

He was able to make an arrangement with the law firm of Shuford, Hodges and Robinson, around the corner on Wall Street. In the morning he typed for the firm on its typewriter. In exchange, in the afternoon he was allowed to use the firm's typewriter to do jobs for paying customers. A year later Daniels borrowed $50, bought a used typewriter and a used mimeograph machine, and opened a business office in Room 27 of the old McIntire Building on College Street in an area that since has been cleared by urban renewal.

There the business prospered. A year or so later Daniels expanded into Room 28. His son, James W., and his daughter, Barbara, both worked in the company, and his wife, Dorothy, labored as office manager and chief typist.

The firm later moved to 342 Merrimon Avenue. By that time Daniels Business Services could afford an electric typewriter and an electric mimeograph machine. Daniels also acquired a used offset press, and he and his son taught themselves how to use it.

The Daniels Business Services, Inc., facility at 15 Rankin Avenue in downtown Asheville today.

In 1955, troubled by a lack of capital and failing health, Daniels sold the company to Dr. Logan Robertson, an Asheville investor who put together the forerunner of the modern conglomerate. He organized the DiSer (Diversified Services) Corp., which owned, among other things, the Daniels operation, the old Manor Hotel, a sports car company, a photo lab, and an aviation firm called Di-Ser Aero.

Prior to his father's death in 1964, James Daniels had served in the Air Force and had attended St. Mary's University in San Antonio, Texas. Later that year James bought the firm from Robertson. In 1969 he acquired Miller Printing Company, known as the company of "firsts"—first offset press, first litho camera, first computerized typesetting. In 1972 he moved his operation to the Miller Printing plant at 15 Rankin Avenue. Miller Printing began business in 1916 and erected the building on Rankin Avenue some eight years later, ranking itself as the largest printing firm in western North

The Daniels Business Services building in 1924 when it was occupied by the Miller Press Inc., the original occupant.

Carolina, Daniels combined the printing, mailing, and answering service operations there.

Daniels Business Services, Inc., which employs 60 people in its various companies, now operates Daniels Graphics, Daniels Answering Service, Daniels Monitoring Service, and Daniels Marketing Services Group.

McGUIRE, WOOD, WORLEY & BISSETTE, P.A.

In 1894 Haywood Parker gave up teaching and became an attorney. The following year he joined Louis M. Bourne, a native of Tarboro, to establish the firm of Bourne and Parker. The partners opened an office at 12 South Court Square, in close proximity to the Buncombe County Courthouse.

The building long since has vanished, but the firm endures. Now named McGuire, Wood, Worley & Bissette, P.A., it has occupied offices in the First Union Bank Building in downtown Asheville since 1967.

Parker and Bourne were joined in 1903 by General Theodore Davidson, who had served as attorney general of North Carolina from 1885 to 1892. He was called General Davidson not because he held military rank, but rather because the custom of the day was to bestow the title on people who had served as the state's attorney general.

Davidson was a partner in the firm until 1911, when he became of counsel. He died in 1930 at the age of 99—still of counsel. Davidson was the forerunner of a number of attorneys who joined the practice, served the legal profession, and left their marks on the community.

One of the most prominent was Silas G. Bernard, who studied law with the firm and passed the bar in 1901. He served as police and fire chief of Asheville from 1905 to 1909, practiced law in Asheville, and then joined the firm in 1932, which at that time was known as Davidson, Bourne and Parker.

Frank M. Parker, son of Haywood Parker, joined the firm in 1936 and it became known as Parker, Bernard and Parker. Frank Parker remained with the firm until he was appointed to the North Carolina Court of Appeals in 1968 by Governor Dan Moore. He has again been associated with the firm as counsel since his retirement from the bench in 1980. Walter R. McGuire, a partner since 1952, served on the State Board of Bar Examiners from 1972 until 1981. James M. Baley, Jr., United States District Attorney from 1953 to 1961, was a partner until 1973, when he was appointed to the North Carolina Court of Appeals by Governor James Holshouser. Richard A. Wood, Jr., joined the firm in 1965, followed by Charles R. Worley in 1971, W. Louis Bissette, Jr., and Douglas O. Thigpen in 1976, Joseph P. McGuire in 1978, and Doris S. Phillips in 1981.

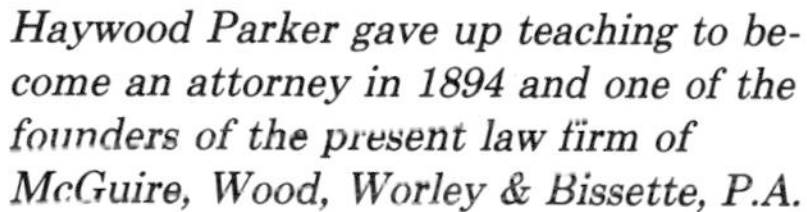

Haywood Parker gave up teaching to become an attorney in 1894 and one of the founders of the present law firm of McGuire, Wood, Worley & Bissette, P.A.

Silas G. Bernard, a member of the firm from 1932 until his death in 1974.

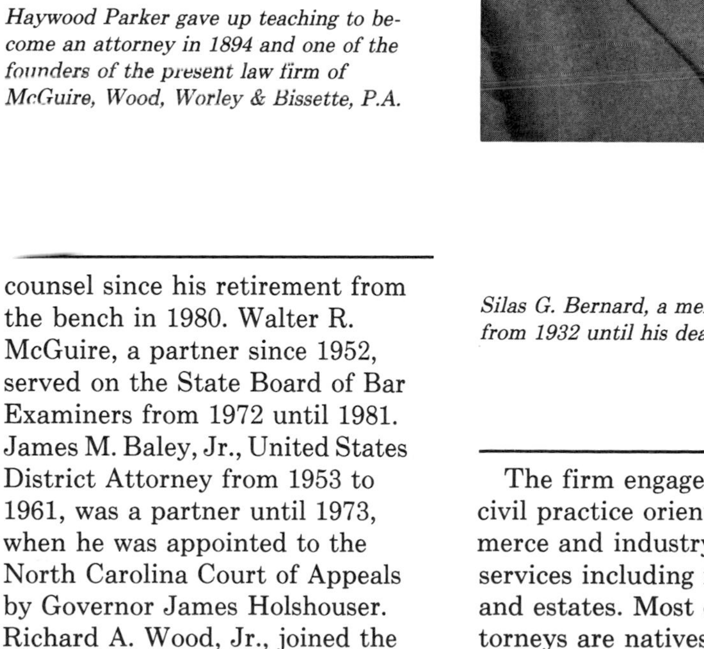

The firm engages in a general civil practice oriented toward commerce and industry and personal services including real property and estates. Most of the firm's attorneys are natives of the area. Its members have been active in community life in many fields through the years, including service by Wood (1971-1975) and Bissette (currently) as mayors of Asheville.

CHRIST SCHOOL

Christ School is artfully situated amid 500 acres of green, rolling fields and a forest of arrow-straight Carolina White Pines in south Buncombe County. It is the only private boys' preparatory school in North Carolina. There, in buildings constructed of biscuit-colored sandstone quarried on the school property, approximately 150 young men in grades 8 through 12 live and study. The education they receive is college preparatory of so high a caliber that few Christ School graduates have any trouble being admitted to the college or university of their choice.

Christ School is affiliated with the Episcopal Church, and students attend evensong services and communion services on Sunday in the school's chapel. However, admission is open to young men of any faith. Although the students are drawn mainly from the Southeast, in 1986 they represented 19 states and 2 foreign countries.

The institution was founded in 1900 by the Reverend Thomas C. Wetmore and his wife. The Reverend Wetmore was pastor of Calvary Episcopal Church in Fletcher, North Carolina, not far from the school. The land was donated by Mrs. Wetmore. The first money received, $1,000, was given by friends in the North. Labor was donated by neighbors.

The school was founded to serve the children of mountain men and women in an area in which public education was lacking. According to *Christ School,* 1902, "The object of the school is to promote the spread of practical Christianity, and to teach young men and women to use their hearts, minds, and hands." It still is today.

The concern with practical, hands-on effort has persisted to this day. Christ School continues to be a self-help facility at which the students do much of the physical labor necessary to maintain the institution. The main thrust of the institution, however, is academic. Students have the opportunity to pursue their studies to the limit of their abilities because of the close proximity of the masters.

As public education in the region improved, Christ School evolved. In 1925 day students and grammar school classes were dropped, leaving the institution with 60 boarding students at the high school level. Today there are 150 boys.

Ownership of the school is held by the self-perpetuating board of directors. Students are divided into grades, called forms. The average class size is small, and teachers are referred to as "masters."

Christ School uses a prefect system under which four seniors are selected to serve as prefects and they are assisted by senior proctors. They provide most of the student leadership on campus. Seniors traditionally play a large role in school government and supervision of the underclassmen.

In addition, Christ School offers a strong sports and recreation program highlighted by a traditional rivalry with Asheville School, another Buncombe County private institution.

Evensong services are held in the chapel of Christ School, which is affiliated with the Episcopal Church.

Christ School in the early 1920s.

STEELCASE INC.

The Stow & Davis North Carolina Division of Steelcase Inc. came into existence in 1973 when the parent corporation expanded its office furniture product offerings into the wood market.

Nearly 60 years before opening its North Carolina facility, Steelcase Inc. was founded as the Metal Office Furniture Co. in Grand Rapids, Michigan, in 1912. It employed 15 people in 8,000 square feet of space. Total sales that first year were $13,000. Among the firm's first products were steel safes and metal wastebaskets. In the years that followed the corporation grew to become the world's leading designer and manufacturer of office furniture, systems furniture, office lighting, and computer software programs aimed at helping planners produce effective and efficient office environments.

The company's name was changed to Steelcase Inc. in 1954. It has led the industry in sales volume since 1968. In recent years the firm's consolidated net sales have been approximately double those of its nearest competitor. It now has a combined (with joint-venture operations) work force of more than 15,000.

Steelcase Inc. works with more than 700 independent dealers, has sales offices or dealerships in 58 countries, and owns 15 million square feet of manufacturing space at 21 manufacturing facilities in nine countries—seven in the United States, six in France, four in Africa, two in Canada, and one each in West Germany and Japan. Annual consolidated net sales for fiscal-year 1986 were $1.4 billion. If publicly held, Steelcase Inc. would rank 248th on the *Fortune* 500 listing of major industrial companies in the United States.

The firm's Asheville operation came about as part of a program to develop new manufacturing facilities in locations outside Grand Rapids. Although Steelcase furniture manufactured here is made with wood, and although western North Carolina produces fine hardwood, proximity to wood sources was not the main reason for locating in the Asheville area, says John R.E. Ruhl, general manager of the company's Asheville operation since 1976. "Climate, the availability of skilled workers, and central location were the key reasons for selecting Asheville," Ruhl says. "If you draw circles 500-700 miles from Asheville, you take in many of the heavily populated and expanding areas in the eastern half of the country."

In 1972 Steelcase Inc. purchased property in a new industrial park located on what once was the old Asheville-Hendersonville airport near Fletcher, North Carolina. The first stage of the plant was opened in September 1973. It had 200,000 square feet of work space and employed 50 people. Two succeeding expansions in 1978 and 1982 provided a total area of 850,000 square feet. Its work force currently totals approximately 800 people.

Steelcase Inc. has become an important part of the Asheville community and plays a leading role in many civic and business undertakings. It has acquired a reputation as a good neighbor. "That's simply a reflection of the way Steelcase operates in all locations," says Ruhl. "It's just a part of the Steelcase culture, which has a heavy focus on people."

The Steelcase Inc. plant located on the site of the old Asheville-Hendersonville airport near Fletcher, North Carolina, a suburb of Asheville.

ASHEVILLE AREA CHAMBER OF COMMERCE

In the waning days of 1897, a group of Asheville businessmen began a series of meetings keyed to a need they believed existed in the community. They wanted a way to present the business point of view in a mountain city growing in size and diversity. On January 12, 1898, approximately 65 businessmen met in the Asheville Club and adopted a constitution and bylaws for the Asheville Board of Trade.

One of the early homes for the Asheville Area Chamber of Commerce was this brick building at 18-28 North Market Street. This photo was taken in 1926.

This attractive fieldstone building at 151 Haywood Street in downtown Asheville is the present home of the chamber.

The names of the first directors were almost a roll call from the city's past. Represented were the Mason, Patton, Alexander, Nichols, Williams, Blair, Jones, and Chapman families—all prominent in Asheville's history. T.S. Morrison, a downtown merchant, was elected chairman, and Charles T. Rawls became the organization's first secretary.

Almost the first order of business was to find a way to counteract a scoundrelly article in *The New York Journal* that alleged that the Biltmore House and Estate was a "complete failure." It was not a failure, and the new Asheville Board of Trade wanted the world to know it.

During the following year the board promoted the organization of the Good Roads Association. It was the first of many betterment organizations the board, and later the chamber, would initiate. Another early campaign by the Asheville Board of Trade came in 1918, when it sponsored a Drink More Milk drive aimed at helping the dairy industry in western North Carolina. On September 22, 1921, the Board of Trade became the Asheville Chamber of Commerce (later the Asheville Area Chamber of Commerce).

The newly renamed group plunged into a major, long-term advertising campaign during the mid-1920s. Both Asheville and Buncombe County were enjoying boom times, real estate values were soaring, and the chamber kept pace with the community. In 1928 the organization played a key role in persuading Dutch industrialists to buy property in Asheville and build the huge Enka rayon mill. The mill provided much-needed jobs and helped establish the area as a textile center.

That same year the chamber organized its annual spring Rhododendron Festival. The festival ended in 1942, a victim of World War II. Another promotion that was started in 1928 was the Mountain Dance & Folk Festival, an annual celebration of folk culture that still is going strong.

In the postwar years the chamber played an increasingly influential role in bringing new industry to the area and in pushing for civic improvements such as a new airport, better schools, and improved water supply facilities. It sought to broaden educational opportunities and enhance the cultural component of the community.

The Asheville Area Chamber of Commerce, to a degree probably not imagined by the men who founded it in 1898, has, indeed, given business leaders a way to express the business point of view, and it has helped lead the community into a better and more rewarding future.

WESTERN CAROLINA UNIVERSITY

The growth of Western Carolina University has been termed "the progress of an idea." The idea, in the words of its founder, Robert Lee Madison, was "to establish the kind of school that our mountain territory needed."

Madison came to western North Carolina in December 1885 to teach in a small school near the Cherokee Indian Reservation. He was only 17 years of age, but already held bachelor's and master's degrees. He was impressed by the bright young people he met and by their industrious parents, but he was distressed by the lack of opportunity for education.

Madison opened Cullowhee High School, predecessor of Western Carolina University, in 1889 in a frame structure unfurnished except for a few heavy benches and a blackboard. In 1893 a Normal Department was established. Students who completed the course received a first-grade teaching certificate valid in any part of the state.

The twentieth century brought numerous changes to the institution. During the 1950s the college began a period of unprecedented growth. One addition was the Graduate School, which was established in 1951. In 1967 full regional university status was achieved. Five years later the college became one of the 16 institutions in the University of North Carolina system.

In 1937 Western Carolina University began to offer resident-credit programs at an extension center in Oteen. These programs were moved to the University of North Carolina's Asheville campus in 1975 and became known as WCU Programs in Asheville. Western Carolina University currently offers a broad array of graduate programs through the UNC Graduate Center in Asheville.

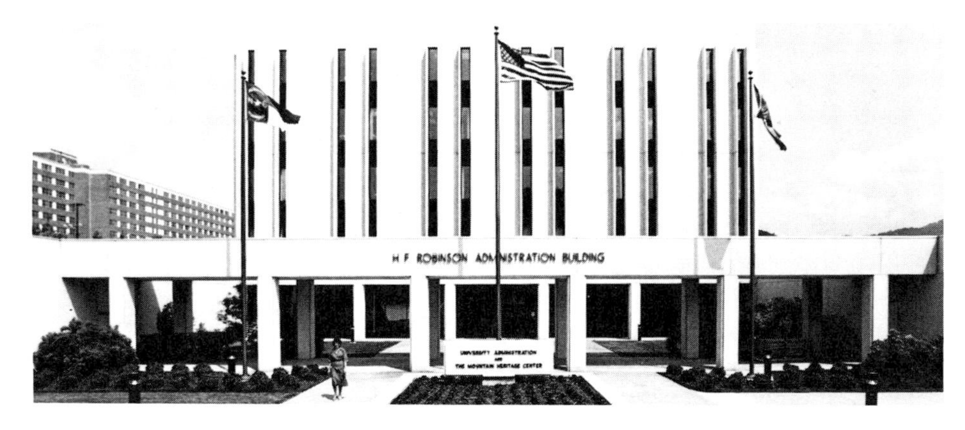

The H.F. Robinson Administration Building houses offices and services previously located in 12 different structures. The building was authorized by the North Carolina Legislature in 1976.

Today the 6,500 students enrolled at Western Carolina University may choose undergraduate studies in computer science, radio and television, parks and recreation management, natural resources management, emergency medical care, engineering technology, environmental health, criminal justice, microelectronics engineering technology, therapeutic recreation, as well as the traditional areas of education, business, arts, and sciences. In addition, new graduate degree programs in diverse fields have widened opportunities for advanced study.

Research and services also have expanded. The Center for Improving Mountain Living, established in 1975, provides domestic and international assistance to governments, agencies, communities, and individuals. The Mountain Heritage Center, founded in 1974, collects, preserves, records, and displays materials, artifacts, and collections related to the history and heritage of western North Carolina. The Fine Arts Center promotes art, theater, and music throughout the region.

Western Carolina University employs about 1,000 people on a full-time basis; its annual payroll is $29 million. The physical plant now comprises 56 academic and residential buildings located on more than 200 acres landscaped with native gardens, parks, and playing fields. The 22,000 individuals who have been awarded degrees from the institution have gone on to play important roles in the professional, business, and civic affairs of the mountain region and the nation.

This frame building, completed in 1889, originally was the entire physical plant for the school that later became Western Carolina University.

ASHEVILLE-BUNCOMBE TECHNICAL COLLEGE

Asheville-Buncombe Technical College lives on the cutting edge of technology, but remains firmly anchored in the history of the area it serves.

The angular modernity of many of the institution's buildings is offset by the nineteenth-century charm of the Smith-McDowell House, the oldest residence in Buncombe County. The home, painstakingly restored, now serves as a museum. Fernihurst, another gracious old residence, houses the school's Human Resources Development program.

Asheville-Buncombe Technical College began with a state bond issue in 1959 that provided $300,000 for planning and site acquisition for a school to be called the Asheville-Buncombe Industrial Education Center. The bond issue was the culmination of efforts of governors Luther Hodges and Terry Sanford, both of whom early on saw the need to improve technical educaton in North Carolina.

Next came the acquisition of a 21-acre tract in south Asheville. On September 1, 1961, classes were held for the first time in the two buildings constructed on the campus. From that point on the institution never looked back. Enrollment increased steadily by 10 percent per year. New buildings were erected and new programs were added on a regular basis. In 1974 the school acquired an addition of 78 acres, site of the former Asheville Catholic High School.

Early in its existence the college was controlled by the Asheville City Board of Education. However, in 1964 the school was deeded to a new, independent board of trustees and was renamed the Asheville-Buncombe Technical Institute.

In December 1969 the school was accredited by the Commission on Colleges of the Southern Association of Colleges and Schools. Ten years later it officially was named the Asheville-Buncombe Technical College.

Today the institution carefully coordinates its curricula to meet the needs of local business and industry. It works closely with area public schools to identify and supply special educational needs. It also offers a varied and popular array of continuing education courses.

The Old World charm of Fernihurst contrasts with the up-to-the-minute atmosphere of the rest of the Asheville-Buncombe Technical College campus. Photo by Sharon Kuhne

Asheville-Buncombe Technical College has become a leader in the training of nurses and law enforcement officers. It is also recognized for its programs in vocational-industrial skills, engineering technology, and business education. Graduates of the college's culinary arts and hospitality programs are much in demand in the local resort area. The institution is also pioneering in the use of computers as industrial tools, such as computer-controlled machine tools.

On September 1, 1975, Harvey Haynes was named president of the college. He succeeded the institution's founding president, Thomas W. Simpson.

In 1985 fall enrollment at Asheville-Buncombe Technical College was a record 2,838 students in degree and diploma programs and approximately 15,000 in continuing education programs. The institution currently is housed in 14 buildings and operates on an annual budget in excess of $11 million.

As modern as the curricula taught at Asheville-Buncombe Technical College is the administration building, called the Simpson Building.

PATRONS

The following individuals, companies, and organizations have made a valuable commitment to the quality of this publication. Windsor Publications and the Western North Carolina Historical Association gratefully acknowledge their participation in *Asheville: Land of the Sky.*

Perry M. Alexander Construction Company
Alliance Carolina Tool & Mold
Appalachian Hall*
Asheville Area Chamber of Commerce*
Asheville-Buncombe Technical College*
The Asheville Citizen-Times Publishing Co.*
Asheville Federal Savings and Loan Association*
Asheville Infectious Disease Consultants, P.A.
The Asheville School*
BASF Corporation Fibers Division*
Beverly-Hanks and Associates*
Brad's Cards 'n More
Christ School*
Thomas L. Codington, P.A.
Mr. and Mrs. Stewart B. Coleman
Daniels Business Services, Inc.*
The Grove Park Inn and Country Club*
Highland Hospital*
Verna McGaughey
McGuire, Wood, Worley & Bissette, P.C.*
Memorial Mission Hospital*
Pepsi-Cola Bottling Co. of Asheville Inc.*
Poncho's La Casita Restaurant
Royal Crown Bottling Co. of Asheville, Inc.*
St. Joseph's Hospital*
Southeastern Container, Inc.
Square D Company*
Steelcase Inc.*
Swannanoa Cleaners, Inc.*
Thoms Rehabilitation Hospital, Inc., of Western North Carolina*
Van Winkle, Buck, Wall, Starnes and Davis, P.A.*
Western Carolina University*

*Partners in Progress of *Asheville: Land of the Sky.* The histories of these companies and organizations appear in Chapter 12, beginning on page 105.

BIBLIOGRAPHY

Allen, Martha Norburn. *Asheville & Land of The Sky.* Charlotte: Heritage House, 1960.

Arthur, John Preston. *Western North Carolina from 1730-1913.* Raleigh: Edwards and Broughton Printing Co., 1914.

Asbury, Francis. *Journal.* New York: Lane & Scott, 1852.

Asheville. Asheville: Chamber of Commerce pamphlet, 1929.

Asheville City Directories, 1887 to present in Pack Memorial Library, Asheville.

Aswell, James R., Julia Willhoit, et al. *God Bless the Devil! Liar's Bench Tales.* Knoxville: University of Tennessee Press, 1983.

Bailey, David C. *Farewell to Valor.* Asheville: Hexagon Co., 1977.

Barrett, John G. "General Sherman's March Through North Carolina." *North Carolina Historical Review,* 42 (1965).

Blackmun, Ora. *Western North Carolina to 1880.* Boone: Appalachian Consortium Press, 1977.

________. *A Spire in the Mountains: The Story of 176 Years of a Church and a Town Growing Together.* Asheville: First Presbyterian Church, 1970.

Bowman, Isaiah. *Forest Physiography.* New York: John Wiley & Sons, 1911.

Camp, Cordelia. *Governor Vance, A Life For Young People.* Designed by Burney Weaver. Asheville: The Stephens Press, 1961.

Chickering, J.W., Jr. "Thermal Belts." *Science,* 1883.

Colton, Henry. *Mountain Scenery.* Raleigh: W.L. Pomeroy, 1859.

Corhram, David H. "Cherokee Pre-History" *North Carolina Historical Review,* 34 (1957).

Dickens, Roy S., Jr. *Cherokee Pre-History—The Pisgah Phase in the Appalachian Summit Region.* Knoxville: University of Tennessee Press, 1976.

Dykeman, Wilma. *The French Broad.* Knoxville: University of Tennessee Press, 1955.

Eller, Ronald D. *Miners, Millhands & Mountaineers.* Knoxville: University of Tennessee Press.

The Floods of 1916. Washington, D.C.: Southern Railway Co., 1917.

Gatewood, William Badgette, Jr. "North Carolina's Role in the Establishment of the Great Smoky Mountains National Park." *North Carolina Historical Review,* 37 (1960).

Goodrich, Frances Louisa. *Mountain Homespun.* New Haven: Yale University Press, 1931.

The Grove Park Inn Story. Asheville: Jack Tar Hotels.

Harshaw, Lou. *Asheville: Places of Discovery.* Laucemont, Ga: Copple House Books, 1980.

Hayes, C. Willard. *The Southern Appalachians.* National Geographic Monographs. No. 10, v.I. New York: 1895.

Helper, Hinton. *Asheville, North Carolina: Nature's Trundle-Bed of Recuperation.* New York: Smith Publishing Co., 1886.

Hope, James Barron. *Sketches of North Carolina, by Ex-Governor Vance Together With Elegiac Ode and Other Poems by J.B. Hope.* Norfolk, Va: The Norfolk Landmark, 1875.

Inscoe, John C. "Mountain Master: Slaveholding in Western North Carolina." *North Carolina Historical Review,* 61 (1984).

Keith, Arthur. "Outlines of Appalachian Structure." *Bulletin of the Geological Society of America,* 1923.

Langley, Joan. *Yesterday's Asheville.* Miami: E.A. Seeman Publishing, 1975.

Lindsey, Thomas H. *Guide Book To Western North Carolina.* Asheville: Randolph-Kerr Printing Co., 1890.

Lounsbury, Carl. "The Building Process in Antebellum North Carolina." *North Carolina Historical Review,* 60 (1982).

McCoy, George W. "Asheville and Thomas Wolfe." *North Carolina Historical Review,* 30 (1953).

Michaux, F.A. *Travels to the Westward of the Allegheny Mountains.* London: 1805.

Mooney, James. *Myths of the Cherokees.* Extract from Nineteenth Annual Report of the Bureau of American Ethnology. Washington, D.C.: 1902.

Morley, Margaret W. *Carolina Mountains.* New York: Houghton, Mifflin Co., 1943.

Morris, Margaret W. "The Completion of the Western North Carolina Railroad: The Politics of Concealment." *North Carolina Historical Review,* Summer (1975).

Newsome, A.R., Ed. "John Brown's Journal of Travel in Western North Carolina in 1795." *North Carolina Historical Review,* 11 (1934).

Newspapers on microfilm at Pack Memorial Library.
Asheville Citizen
Asheville Citizen-Times
Asheville Daily Citizen
Asheville Gazette-News
Asheville Times

North Carolina Division of Archives & History. Raleigh. Especially for Brown, Clingman, Gash, and Vance papers, and records on soldiers, pensions, hotel accounts, citizenship and naturalization records, school records, slave lists, and lists of Asheville city and Buncombe County officials.

Pack Memorial Library, Asheville. Vertical files on Asheville and Buncombe County.

Palerdon, Phillip Shaw. *Victims.* Knoxville: University of Tennessee Press, 1984.

Patton, James W. "Glimpse of North Carolina in the Writings of Northern and Foreign Travelers." *North Carolina Historical Review,* 45 (1968).

Phifer, Edward W., Jr. "Religion in the Raw: Cyclone Mack in Burke County." *North Carolina Historical Review,* 48 (1971).

Reid, Richard. "A Test Case of the 'Crying Evil': Desertion among North Carolina Troops During the Civil War." *North Carolina Historical Review,* 58 (1981).

Riley, Jack. *Carolina Power & Light 1908-1958.* Raleigh: Edwards and Broughton County, 1958.

Rulfs, Donald J. "The Theater in Asheville from 1879 to 1931." *North Carolina Historical Review,* 36 (1959).

Sawyer, Harriet Adams. *Souvenir of Asheville N.C. or The Sky-land.* St. Louis: Nixon Jones Printing Co., 1892.

Shackford, James A. "David Crockett and North Carolina." *North Carolina Historical Review,* 28 (1951).

Shirley, Franklin Ray. *Zeb Vance, Tarheel Spokesman.* Charlotte: McNally & Loftin, 1962.

Simpson, Marcus B., Jr. "The Letters of John S. Cairns to William Brewster, 1887-1895." *North Carolina Historical Review,* 55 (1978).

Sondley, Foster A. *A History of Buncombe County.* Asheville: Advocate Printing Co., 1930.

Sterling, Robert B. "The Plank Road Movement in North Carolina, Parts I and II." *North Carolina Historical Review,* 16 (1939).

Terrell, Robert. *Grandpa's Town.* Asheville: 1978.

Tiernan, Frances Fisher [Christian Reid]. *The Land of the Sky.* New York: Appleton & Co., 1876.

Tucker, Glenn. *Zeb Vance: Champion of Personal Freedom.* Indianapolis: Bobbs-Merrill, 1965.

Vance, Zebulon B. *The Scattered Nation.* Raleigh: Alfred Williams & Co., 1928.

Van Noppen, Ina W. and John J. *Western North Carolina Since the Civil War.* Boone: Appalachian Consortium Press, 1973.

Ver Steeg, Karl. "Some Features of Appalachian Peneplanes." *Pan American Geologist,* LIII, LIV (1930).

Waldrow, Holman. *With Pen and Camera Thru the Land of the Sky.* Portland: Chisholm Brothers, 1911.

Webb, Charles Aurelius. *Fifty-eight Years in Asheville.* Asheville: The Asheville Citizen-Times Inc., 1948.

Williamson, William B. and Kay Dixon. *The Davidson and Allied Families Originating in North Carolina: Davidson Family, Vance Family, Brank Family and Howell Family.* Gastonia: William Gaston Chapters, D.A.R., 1956.

Willis, Bailey. "Round About Asheville." *National Geographic Magazine,* 1888-1890.

Wolfe, Thomas C. *Look Homeward, Angel.* New York: Charles Scribner, 1929.

Wright, Frank. "The Older Appalachians of the South." Denison University Bulletin, XXXI (1931).

Zeigler, Wilbur Gleason, and Ben S. Grossup. *The Heart of the Alleghenies: or Western North Carolina.* Cleveland: 1883.

INDEX

PARTNERS IN PROGRESS INDEX

GENERAL INDEX
Italicized numbers indicate illustrations